talent

Awakening in Hyper-Competitive Environments

Dr Alkesh Vyas

Copyright Notice

A catalogue record for this work is available from the National Library of Australia

Non-fiction/Economics, Finance, Business & Management

ISBN(sc): 978-0-6489210-3-5

ISBN(e): 978-0-6489210-4-2

Dedication

With deep gratitude and love for my parents,
Dahyalal (Batuk) and Shardaben Vyas

TABLE OF CONTENTS

LIST OF TABLES

LIST OF FIGURES

Preface

Throughout a career that spans over 30 years and four different continents, I have been witness to and experienced differences in cultural diversity, ways of operation and management styles from diverse industries and corporate cultures. I have observed the suffocation of creativity that arises from the adoption of standard processes that demotivate staff (agents), as well as the difference in treatment of agents at various organisational levels. Suffocation of creativity has undoubtedly resulted in knowledge leakage in addition to the creation of stress and frustration for agents who are unable to change careers or move organisations due to a lack of opportunities and skills portability. These experiences led me to question: 'How can an organisation create conditions that not only allow it to retain knowledge but further assists the organisation to achieve long-term sustainability through creativity and innovation?'

Following years of contemplation, through this case study, I have had the opportunity to provide some answers to this problem. Creativity and innovation are essential for organisations to ensure sustained competitive and comparative advantage, which makes it the responsibility of each agent within organisational structures. The structural space model Fig. 8.2 in Part Eight section 59 will help organisations facilitate creativity and innovation. Further integration can assist in an informed view and awareness of the effects of interactions on adaptive leadership, creativity and innovation.

Introduction

This book introduces strategies to operationalise adaptive leadership, in the process awakening talent within organisations. There is a perception in academic and business communities that leadership has close links with intellectual capital management, which has consequences for social capital and poses significant competitive risks to organisations. Due to its significance and importance for global economies, the case study focuses on the resources sector. In the global economy, increasingly volatile competition also creates an environment of **hyper-competition**[1] in which organisational benefits rapidly grow and diminish[2] to make these environments dynamic, unpredictable and hostile.[3] Additionally, the resources sector depends on high levels of fixed capital investment, relatively fixed natural resources, and fluctuations and shortages of labour skills. Thus, fundamental challenges and imperatives for leadership strategies that build and retain both intellectual and social capital are examined.

A single resources organisation formed the case study basis, including face-to-face interviews to canvass the views and experiences of participants on creativity, innovation, interactions, managed socialisation and leadership within the organisation. Three themes emerged:

1. operationalisation,
2. interactions and
3. social capital.

These themes collectively describe the enablers and barriers to creativity and innovation as well as the influence of adaptive leadership. Through this case study, a model sequentially develops that addresses the need for 'structural space' as an area of creative tension and innovation, which arises from stresses within cybernetic leadership processes and the need for creativity and innovation.

A range of strategies beneficial for organisations that wish to embrace creative and innovative solutions and develop a sustained competitive and comparative advantage are provided. These strategies include:

- the facilitation and enablement of social interactions or managed socialisation,
- the development of a common communication language,
- creation of independent departments to oversee the collation, analysis, implementation and reward of creative and innovative ideas and
- equipping people with the right skills and attitudes.

Part One: Challenge

1. Overview

This case study investigated the processes to operationalise adaptive leadership through principles of complexity leadership. This case study aimed to better understand the effects of adaptive leadership on intellectual capital management and social capital of organisations in the natural resources sector globally, with a specific focus on those organisations based in Western Australia.

Considerable frustration and stress result from social capital erosion, poor intellectual capital management practices and inadequate leadership strategies. Frustration and stress can result in lost opportunities to benefit from internally generated creativity and innovation, especially when there is a loss of informal interactions among organisational agents. With the effect of voluntary employee turnover on the performance of organisations, referred to as the pied-piper effect, that occurs when teams or groups of employees leave organisations.[1] There is a further effect of knowledge leakage that results from employee turnover and the subsequent loss of organisational human capital.[2]

A complexity leadership lens is useful to identify gaps in leadership strategies and to provide a better interpretation of adaptive leadership. As industry identifies and addresses leadership gaps, it will help to generate knowledge of practices that lead to a competitive resources industry. Additionally, knowledge assets assist in the awareness of how and why organisations function in the ways they do and how contextual conditions affect organisations.[3]

2. Background

Natural resource mining has long been crucial to Western Australia's social and economic development. Mining comprises of an array of activities, which include minerals extraction, petroleum extraction and services to mining, mining-related manufacturing, electricity and gas production activities.[1] In the first decade of the 2000s, the resources industry experienced a long-predicted deficit of workers with the skills required to perform highly specialised tasks, which was due in part to a maturing population.[2] Shortage of workers led to an increased dependence on contributions from knowledge workers, who possessed a high degree of distinctive transferable skills that they applied to critical challenges to organisational sustainability.[3] Knowledge workers apply their expertise and learning and are generally responsible for fostering creativity and innovation in organisations through the utilisation of their acquired knowledge and experience.[4]

In 2011, the Minerals Council of Australia predicted that Australia required a further 86,000 personnel to boost the workforce of 216,000.[5] Although there was rapid job growth in the resources industry,[6] by November 2014, direct employment in the minerals industry remained at 208,200.[7] However, the Minerals Council stated that the resources sector in Australia experienced a skills shortage rather than a labour shortage.[8] Despite the existence of a well-skilled workforce, with greater than 34 per cent possessing a tertiary level qualification, to minimise production disruption, resource organisations incurred extra onsite costs to train individuals.[9]

During boom times, to meet the demands of the resources sector, there is an increased reliance on knowledge workers who use tacit skills and knowledge to understand processes, generate concepts and provide necessary guidance for other highly specialised production and operational tasks.[10] Tacit knowledge and skills cannot be systematised or collected as they are:

- not visible in their application,
- not transferable,
- not verbalised,
- intricate and
- context-specific.[11]

Knowledge workers, however, apply tacit skills and knowledge at their discretion, which means organisations rely on the functional participation or favourable citizenship behaviour of such workers to operate effectively.[12] The efficacy of knowledge workers lies in their inclination, capability to exploit, integrate personal and organisational knowledge to be creative and innovative in organisations.[13] Thus, the effectiveness of knowledge workers is critical in environments that dynamically change as well as in knowledge-intensive industries in which creativity and its conversion into marketable innovation remain crucial. Organisational agents drive value creation to make culture, values and vision critical.[14] However, knowledge workers seek employability rather than employment,[15] may have substantially different expectations of their employers and thus tend to change jobs frequently. In the process, knowledge workers create social capital and knowledge erosion in organisations.

The individual experience and tacit knowledge of knowledge workers are crucial assets for the continuous improvement and innovation of companies, which coexist with the regular work responsibilities of employees.[16] Concurrently, knowledge workers have transferrable skills, which makes them attractive to a range of organisations.[17] Therefore, organisations that recognise knowledge workers as being crucial assets need to implement steps to retain these employees to safeguard their competitiveness and growth.[18] Thus, the resources sector can align training with labour needs to address skills shortages; however, with a mature population, this is a challenge.[19]

Tension and competition require long-term knowledge management initiatives that consider dynamic environmental changes.[20] Therefore organisationally, it is time critical to understand strategic gaps that can underpin knowledge gaps,[21] which requires leaders to have the capacity to internalise organisational knowledge into a core advantage.[22] Labour skills shortage make it vital to meet such challenges through appropriate management systems to ensure organisations effectively utilise comparative and competitive advantages from organic creativity and innovation.

A competitive advantage exists at the heart of organisational performance in increasingly global competitive markets.[23] It stems from the varied activities performed throughout the organisation's value chain, which drives and supports value.[24] Competitive advantage generated from internal organisational resources and capabilities is more sustainable than that based solely on a product and market position,[25] with long-term corporate value created through effective management of intangibles.[26] Organisational intangibles include:

- proficiency,
- experience,
- trademarks,
- status,
- competencies,
- internal and external connections and
- employee innovativeness.[27]

Although critical for generating new knowledge, intangibles such as creativity and innovation remain challenging to measure, fundamentally unpredictable, with uncertain outcomes.[28]

3. Vacancies

In the mid-to the late 2000s, due to rapid demand growth from the mining industry, Australia's labour market experienced an excess of demand over supply of particular categories of skills, such as tradespersons and professionals.[1] Low population growth, a mature labour force and a reduction in activities to train workers and internalise knowledge exacerbated this shortage.[2] Table 1.1 demonstrates selected occupational changes in skilled vacancies across Australia.

Table 1.1: Vacancies—selected industry groups (Australia) [3]

Industry Group	Australia statistics released in February '000s				2010 -2020 Δ%
	2010	2014	2018	2020	
Mining	5.2	5.0	5.1	6.5	25.0
Manufacturing	12.3	8.0	12.4	12.2	-0.8
Construction	13.4	13.9	14.5	16.6	23.9
Transport	5.6	4.5	6.5	7.5	33.9
Financial	8.6	9.1	10.3	11.9	38.4
Scientific	19.1	15.4	24.6	26.3	37.7
Retail	11.0	12.3	22.1	18.9	71.8
Education	4.0	2.6	6.8	7.7	92.5

As demonstrated in Table 1.1, demand for skilled workers within the mining (resources) sector remained steady from 2010 to 2018 increasing in 2020, with 25 per cent of total jobs unfilled, which also indicates a continued shortage of required skills. Downstream associated industries also reflected this demand and shortage with vacancies filled in transport (33.9%) and financial (38.4%). Vacancy increases also occurred in construction (23.9%), scientific and technical (37.7%), retail (71.8%) and education (92.5%), with a static manufacturing sector.

At the peak of the resources sector boom in 2011, skilled vacancy rates increased as industries across all sectors scrambled to satisfy the demand for goods and services. Since 2013, vacancy rates have stabilised to 2010 pre-boom activity levels, with a ramp-down of production activities from industries and resource organisations, particularly for iron ore to maintain a steady resource to supply primary markets.

Table 1.2: Vacancies—selected industry groups (Canada)[4]

Industry Group	Canadian statistics released in January '000s				2016 -2019 $\Delta\%$
	2016	2017	2018	2019	
Mining	2.3	5.4	6.2	4.6	95.1
Manufacturing	33.5	42.3	53.1	50.0	49.4
Construction	27.0	33.0	41.2	41.0	51.7
Transport	18.2	27.1	32.9	28.7	57.9
Financial	24.5	22.1	23.2	21.8	-10.9
Scientific	29.6	28.2	35.5	36.8	24.4
Retail	52.4	56.7	62.3	71.7	36.7
Education	11.4	13.2	14.3	14.7	28.8

By way of comparison, Table 1.2 indicates that demand for skilled workers within the mining (resources) sector in Canada also remained strong from 2016 to 2019, with an increase in total jobs of 95.1 per cent. Downstream associated industries reflected this demand and shortage for workers, predominantly with increased vacancies across all major industry groups. The unavailability of Canadian data for 2010–2015 makes a comparison to other geographical locations not possible for that period.

Table 1.3: Vacancies—selected industry groups (United Kingdom)[5]

Industry Group	United Kingdom statistics released in May '000s				2010 -2020 Δ%
	2010	2014	2018	2020	
Mining	1.0	2.0	1.0	1.0	0.0
Manufacturing	30.0	47.0	60.0	33.0	10.0
Construction	10.0	20.0	23.0	13.0	30.0
Transport	18.0	23.0	39.0	19.0	5.6
Financial	30.0	37.0	39.0	22.0	-26.7
Scientific	35.0	59.0	77.0	43.0	22.9
Retail	92.0	117.0	131.0	66.0	-28.3
Education	51.0	50.0	48.0	32.0	-37.3

Table 1.3 illustrates that demand for skilled workers within the mining (resources) sector in the United Kingdom remained steady from

2010 to 2020, with no increase in total jobs. Downstream associated industries reflected this demand and shortage for workers, predominantly with increased or unfilled vacancies across all major industry groups.

4. Globalisation

The vacancy statistics from Australia, Canada and the United Kingdom highlight the global problem of skills deficits, which create increased demand and competition for skills and expertise from global economies and place pressure on organisations to retain knowledge.[1] In addition to the management of their internal resources, which includes skill shortages and resources supply and demand, organisations face external environmental challenges and uncertainties. For example, a currency exchange risk emerges when the Australian dollar strengthens or weakens against the US dollar. As a commodity currency, the Australian dollar traditionally decreases when global commodity prices fall. For example, in 2014, the Australian dollar weakened to an average of 90 US cents, which shielded producers to some extent from a fall in commodity prices.[2]

Globalisation comprises the:

- financial,
- legislative,
- societal,
- cultural,

- constitutional,
- technological and
- physical interrelationships.

These pervade geographic borders and boundaries,[3] which can result in an economy-wide disruption as evident through the 2007–2008 Global Financial Crisis (GFC). Globalisation is also the unique squeezing of time and space, which results from political, economic and cultural pressures, and an increase in the integration of social and cultural norms.[4]

Intellectual capital management is complex for organisations that operate and interconnect globally,[5] with challenges that relate to cultural complexity, human resources, organisational structures and increased competition.[6] Interconnections between corporations or organisations in an environment of extended global supply chains remain crucial when the balance of power between organisations and the communities they serve increasingly favours organisations.

Raised shareholder, as well as other stakeholder expectations for organisations to be socially responsible, generates and places external pressure on organisations in the resources sector to support their local industries and communities. Often referred to as an organisation's social licence[7] or a triple bottom line approach,[8] in which organisations respond to issues beyond their minimum economic, technical and legal requirements.[9]

Organisations that operate globally face substantial challenges when they administer strategies across different cultures and business practices, which expose them to inconsistent information between their stated policies and actual behaviours.[10] Organisational ethical behaviour is an essential characteristic of corporate social responsibility (CSR) because it indicates an organisation's seriousness to act responsibly and prevent injury to stakeholders and displays respect for individuals' moral rights. [11] CSR in the natural resources sector remains controversial as a result of several incidents that demonstrated corporate disregard for human rights and the environment in pursuit of profits.[12] Recent examples include the Deepwater Horizon BP disaster[13] and the BHP Brazil Samarco Mine dam disaster.[14]

In the global economy, hyper-competitiveness allows organisations to supply at lower prices to the detriment of marginal producers and does not occur as a coercive tactic used to force marginal producers out of the market.[15] Established organisations can build stock that drives down the price of resources and force marginal producers to realign costs to survive.[16] In recent times, these economic pressures have resulted in the closure of some high-cost mines, frozen pay and conditions as well as staff redundancies.

5. Migration

As a source of skilled workforce, knowledge acquisition can occur through interstate or overseas migration. Across all Australian states, Western Australia recorded a gradual increase of net interstate migration from 2,100 persons in 2003–2004 to 8,000 persons in 2012–2013.[1] Additionally, the Temporary Work (skilled) visa (subclass 457) was a significant means to attract overseas skilled labour to bridge skills gaps because it allowed, 'skilled workers to come to Australia and work for an approved business for up to four years... A business can sponsor someone for this visa if they cannot find an Australian citizen or permanent resident to do the skilled work.'[2]

The Australian government terminated the Temporary Work visa on 18 April 2017, replacing it from March 2018 with a short-term and a medium-term stream Temporary Skill Shortage visa. The short-term stream permits work in Australia for up to two years. The medium-term stream allows for four years with potential eligibility for permanent residency after a three-year stay.

The use of foreign workers to fill job vacancies on temporary visas persists as a short-term strategy with broader long-term social outcomes.[3] The Canadian International Council[4] recommend that the use of temporary workers should only be a short-term strategy because of its adverse long-term social consequences for communities. The Canadian International Council report focuses on Canada's rich natural resource endowment to understand how Canada manages its natural resource wealth and examines practices from countries similarly rich in natural resources. As shown in Table 1.4, Canada and Australia both have abundant natural resource reserves and face similar geographical, infrastructural, skills and innovation challenges.

Similar environmental challenges make the questions addressed by the Canadian International Council relevant to the Australian natural resource sector. For example, the question of how wealth in resources can be managed and improved sustainably for current and future generations is relevant for both Canada and Australia. The report stated that Canada should use Australian research as both countries face similar labour skills shortages.

Table 1.4 illustrates the closeness and overall global resource production ranks for Canada, Australia and the United Kingdom.

Union movements in Australia campaigned against the Temporary Work Skilled visa claiming that the usage of workers on this visa class creates downward pressure on wages, exploits workers and lowers occupational health and safety standards.[5] The dependence on temporary workers also eliminates organisational pressure to be creative and innovative.[6]

Table 1.4: Global production[7]

Mineral	Australia	% Share	Canada	% Share	United Kingdom	% Share
Aluminium	6	2.50	3	4.70	38	0.10
Coal	5	6.30	13	0.70	39	0.03
Copper	6	4.40	12	2.60	-	-
Diamond	5	9.35	3	15.51	-	-
Gold	2	9.34	5	5.49	-	-
Gravel	-	-	-	-	6	5.70
Iron Ore	1	30.80	9	1.80	-	-
Natural Gas	7	3.24	5	4.13	22	1.01
Nickel	6	6.65	5	8.08		
Petroleum	31	0.40	5	5.00	20	1.10
Rock	-	-	-	-	3	10.50
Salt	5	4.80	7	3.80	12	1.70
Titanium	4	8.10	1	19.80	-	-
Uranium	4	11.10	1	13.05	-	-
Zinc	3	8.90	10	2.40	-	-

(Header spanning: Country rank December 2018)

Table 1.5 presents Net Overseas Migration (NOM) statistics for Australia. It shows that NOM contributed to an increase in the Western Australia skilled workforce of 9.0 per cent of the total NOM numbers in 2019 and 69.8 per cent of the total permanent and temporary skilled visas granted during the 2019 calendar year.[8]

Table 1.5: Net overseas migration (Australia)[9]

	NOM	%	NOM (+)	%	NOM (-)	%
State or territory 2019						
Western Australia						
	18,860	9.0	47,930	9.0	-29,070	9.0
All territories Australia						
	210,660	100.0	533,530	100.0	-322,870	100.0
Groupings and visa 2019						
Temporary Work Skilled visa						
	146,710	69.8	333,150	79.7	-186,440	89.8
Permanent Work Skilled visa						
	63,440	30.2	84,610	20.3	-21,170	10.2
Total	**210,150**	**100.0**	**417,760**	**100.0**	**-207,610**	**100.0**

Note: Plus sign (+) represents arrivals, minus sign represents departures.

Temporary workers can create adverse long-term consequences[10] as the over-dependence on migration does not address the cause of skills shortages, but creates long-term social difficulties.[11] Most organisations face a dynamic and complex competitive landscape[12] as a result of globalisation and technological advances.[13] Economic factors dynamically generate change, with the need to deliver quality information and data promptly.[14] Therefore, innovation and rapid knowledge production are essential for organisational existence, competitive advantage and sustainability.[15]

Table 1.6: Net overseas migration (Canada) [16]

	NOM	%	NOM (+)	%	NOM (-)	%
Jul 2016 – Jun 2017						
New movement	205,387	61.9	272,666	65.3	-67,279	78.5
Returning individuals	39,107	11.8	39,107	9.4	–	–
Net temporary movement	-18,414	-5.5	–	–	-18,414	21.5
Net non-permanent residents	105,988	31.9	105,988	25.4	–	–
Total	**332,068**	**100.0**	**417,761**	**100.0**	**-85,693**	**100.0**
Jan 2017 – Dec 2017						
New movement	219,208	66.0	286,487	68.6	-67,279	78.5
Returning individuals	39,107	11.8	39,107	9.4	–	–
Net temporary movement	-18,414	-5.5	–	–	-18,414	21.5
Net non-permanent residents	139,869	42.1	139,869	33.5	–	–
Total	**379,770**	**114.4**	**465,463**	**111.4**	**-85,693**	**100.0**

Note: Plus sign (+) represents arrivals, minus sign (-) represents departures.

Table 1.6 presents NOM statistics for Canada. NOM contributed to an increase of 332,068 individuals in the period July 2016 – June 2017 and 379,770 visas granted in 2017 calendar year.[17]

Table 1.7 presents NOM statistics for the United Kingdom. For the year 2017, NOM contributed an increase of 282,000 people, 81,000 of whom arrived for work-related purposes and 172,000 for educational purposes.[18]

Table 1.7: Net overseas migration (United Kingdom) [19]

2017	NOM	%	NOM (+)	%	NOM (-)	%
British	-46,000	-16.3	80,000	12.7	-126,000	36.1
European Union	101,000	35.8	240,000	38.0	-139,000	39.8
Non-European Union	227,000	80.5	311,000	49.3	-84,000	24.1
Total	**282,000**	**100.0**	**631,000**	**100.0**	**-349,000**	**100.0**
Main reason						
Work	81,000	28.7	269,000	42.6	-188,000	53.9
Study	172,000	61.0	191,000	30.3	-19,000	5.4
Various	29,000	10.3	171,000	27.1	-142,000	40.7
Total	**282,000**	**100.0**	**631,000**	**100.0**	**-349,000**	**100.0**

Note: Plus sign (+) represents arrivals, minus sign (-) represents departures.

Data shown in the three tables bases the Australian (Table 1.5) and the United Kingdom (Table 1.7) statistics entirely on NOM, whereas Canadian data in Table 1.6 combines with net temporary movement figures, which include work permit holders, study permit holders and refugee claimants.

6. Complexity Leadership Overview

Complexity leadership theory focuses on dynamic adaptive behaviours of interdependent agents who interact within systems under conditions of internal and external pressure. Complexity leadership theory argues that the future of systems lies in the patterns of internal agential interplays that occur within systems and result in behavioural as well as attitudinal changes. Thus, internal agential interactions can enact adaptive leadership and encourage the adaptivity of organisations.[1] Due to significant resource constraints, as well as the volatility of internal and external contextual factors, complexity leadership theory is a useful lens with which to examine the resources sector.

Complexity theory recognises the intricacy of social processes in organisations that cannot attribute to single agents. Leadership is primarily a system phenomenon that results from informal interactions between organisational agents.[2] Conventional views of leadership have a cybernetic focus, in which leaders regulate and control organisational behaviour to achieve results.[3] Cybernetic leadership arises from individual acts of influence rather than from complex interactions between agents.[4] Thus, such leadership overlooks the importance of unpredictability in agential interplays, as leaders cannot easily coerce agents to perform mechanically.[5]

Many organisations in the developed world operate as knowledge-intensive organisations because of the often turbulent and dynamic global environment in which intangible assets such as brands, intellectual property (IP) and relationships act as key value drivers.[6] In these organisations, knowledge creation occurs through a process of informal agential interaction.[7] Thus, organisations become dependent on other factors, including trust and organisational culture,[8] which highlights a significant link between intellectual capital management and complexity leadership.

7. Corporate Social Responsibility

Relationships between global organisations with complex global supply chains and their moral consciences require careful examination because of the imbalance of power between organisations and communities. CSR is the alignment of business operations with social values, where organisations consider and integrate the interests of stakeholders with organisational policies and actions. To achieve business success, social, environmental and financial benefits become a fundamental element of corporate commitment to positively influence society, which society commonly refers to as the triple bottom line approach.

Social responsibility by organisations is a commitment to the improvement of community welfare through discretionary business practices and the contribution of corporate resources.[1] However, organisations that operate in multiple countries have significant difficulty in implementing corporate policies across diverse cultures and business practices. Additionally, conducting operations in various countries exposes organisations to inconsistencies between CSR stated policies and actual practices.[2]

CSR reflects social necessities and consequences of achievements, which consist of explicit policies and practices and reflects organisational obligations to create societal good. Thus, some organisations believe that their association with good causes effectively markets their corporate identity.[3] A commitment of CSR to ethical corporate responsibility also signals to stakeholders that an organisation intends to avert social harm and injury, respect the moral rights of agents and to act with integrity and justice.

Because profit is the principal motivation for organisations in the resources sector, any benefit for local Indigenous stakeholders is understood to be a collateral windfall for them. Thus, Indigenous employment programs that some organisations operate do not necessarily reflect their core values. While employment programs might demonstrate the appearance of socially and politically acceptable conduct, there is often little thought given to how such programs run. As such, many companies treat CSR as a public relations or media exercise and publish social responsibility reports in their annual statements or as separate sustainability reports.[4]

The social, cultural, economic and political conditions of a country also influence the CSR initiatives of organisations operating within those contexts.[5] Social responsibility exists at the crossover of organisational culture and social expectations. In part, the notion of social responsibility originates in the conformity between value systems and structures prevalent in organisations and their environments. As such, business, governmental, legal and social agents operate in compliance with some measure of mutual responsiveness, interdependency, choice and capacity.[6]

Explicit social accountability refers to corporate policies that assume societal interest and communicate responsibility. Whereas implicit social responsibility consists of corporate norms, values and rules that result in requirements to address stakeholder issues and define proper agential obligations. Consequently, institutional frameworks change and raise new incentives for organisations to position themselves within broader systems of responsibility that become standardised due to the legitimacy of such frameworks. However, organisations only consider practices to be legitimate if they exist as best practice, which results in the replication of external structures within organisations.[7]

Many advocates of CSR argue that a long-term operations focus provides more comprehensive benefit than a short-term profit focus. Although, critics counter that CSR distracts organisations from a primary economic focus and that CSR exists primarily as a feel-good program.[8]

Consequently, agency theory dictates that managers have a fiduciary responsibility as agents of shareholders to maximise returns, and to spend money on anything else amounts to a breach of trust. Therefore, appointing agents to act on behalf of principals requires trust under fragmentary situations,[9] which makes trust a foundation of agency theory. Conversely, agents vital to organisational survival or success also act as stakeholders, with organisations that attend to stakeholder interests outperforming organisations that do not. Thus, stakeholder theory underscores the fundamental idea behind the notion of sustainable conduct.[10]

Stakeholder theory proposes that the long-term value of an organisation rests primarily on the knowledge, abilities and commitment of its agents and its relationships with stakeholders.[11] Thus, with a clear link between job satisfaction and CSR,[12] organisations that have conflicting values cannot be socially responsible. Such conflicts become evident when organisations adopt risk exposure strategies for environmental disasters; for example, the Deepwater Horizon BP disaster and Hungary's Red River toxic sludge.[13]

Unbalanced resource distribution throughout the resources sector allows organisations to capitalise on their strengths and use them as a competitive advantage. However, most CSR efforts pit business interests against societal interests, which makes them unproductive. Therefore, organisations should adopt CSR strategies appropriate to individual strengths, with four common reasons for participation:

- moral obligation,
- sustainability,
- licence to operate and
- reputation.

Rather than a cost, constraint or charitable deed, organisations can utilise social responsibility as a potent source of innovation and competitive advantage

Organisations can organically generate knowledge and innovative capability or acquire it inorganically.[14] While organisations in the resource sector employ considerable innovative technologies and modes of operation, much of these technologies and best practices have been developed and integrated within externally procured equipment or services.[15] Consequently, organisations should organically harness and improve on their knowledge and innovative capabilities to become more competitive. Although organically harnessing presents some challenges, it is crucial because most organisations are unable to capitalise on the skills and knowledge resident within their workforce.

8. Summary

Strategies to operationalise adaptive leadership in organisations to increase effectiveness, productivity, staff satisfaction, staff retention, global competitiveness and sustainability are presented. Adaptive leadership strategies can benefit other sectors that seek to achieve sustainability through a highly skilled workforce as well as a competitive advantage through effective leadership and intellectual capital management practices.

Hyper-competitive environments challenge organisations and the markets in which they operate to become increasingly intricate with short life cycles. Due to the reliance of knowledge-intensive organisations on the expertise of their staff, intangibles become essential value creators. Thus, the need to foster creativity and effectively deploy and internalise developing knowledge becomes critical.

This chapter provides a context and background to the case study sector and details its significance for Australian and global resources. Various sources highlight the importance of the resources sector and the impact of skilled labour shortages on Australia and the global economy. With a homogenous and global nature of products and processes, the acquisition of creativity and innovation from the external mind and the transient nature of labour skills remain prevalent in the sector. Additionally, the Australian resources sector faces environmental challenges which influence its competitiveness, including global commodity prices, currency exchange rates and delays from Indigenous title claims.[1]

Part Two: The Resources Sector

9. Western Australia

Extractive industries represent the 'beginning of the beginning'–the initial stage in the basic production circuit and in the web of global production networks that make up the global economy of non-renewable natural resources i.e. materials created and stored in nature through complex biophysical processes over vast periods of time.[1]

This chapter discusses innovation in the Western Australia resources sector and examines stages within a typical mine life cycle. The resources sector in Western Australia exists as a complex and dynamic system that faces significant external risks evolving through the entry, exit and transformation of agents leading to challenges within organisations. An increase in skilled labour shortages in this sector fuels and attracts a transient mobile workforce which possesses functional knowledge and skills essential to work in challenging environmental conditions.

The natural resources sector dominates the Western Australian economy, with mining and mining-related industries (excluding electricity supply) contributing an estimated average of 20.9 per cent ($12.8 billion) annually to Gross State Product (GSP) from 1995–1996 to 1999–2000.[2] Additionally, 'the value of Western Australia's mineral and petroleum industry in 2014 reached just over $114 billion'.[3] With new developments and greenfield investments since 2000, GSP contribution has significantly increased, with an estimated annual average of 26.7 per cent ($25.9 billion) from 2001–2002 to 2005–2006,[4] with the Western Australian GSP for 2013–2014 recorded as approximately $237 billion[5] and 2016-17 recorded as approximately $261 billion.[6]

Because resource organisations operate globally, to be sustainable they need the ability to compete in global markets.[7] With many foreign-owned organisations in the local sector, head office and management share engineering expertise and local experts share their environmental knowledge. Thus, there is a high likelihood of cross-border knowledge spill over between foreign-owned organisations and their parent countries, and vice versa.[8] Due to falling commodity prices, resource companies continue to undertake revaluations of capital projects and further investment in the sector. However, there is an expectation that the resources sector will continue to dominate the Western Australian economy, with significant investment as estimated by the Department of Mines and Petroleum (DMP).[9]

As at March 2015, Western Australia had an estimated $179 billion worth of resource projects under construction or in the committed stage of development, with a further $118 billion allocated to planned or possible projects in coming years.

A consequence of globalisation occurred in 2014–2015 when Western Australia experienced sudden falls in the market prices of mined commodities such as iron ore. The drastic drop in price was predominantly due to established resource organisations oversupplying the market, which forced junior to mid-tier miners to shed staff and shelve projects. Shedding staff then led to social capital erosion for these organisations as well as increased future adaptive challenges.

Generally, mid-tier mining organisations have market values of between US$500 million and US$5 billion,[10] whereas junior mining organisations have market values of less than US$500million with market values of over US$5 billion for top-tier mining organisations (see Table 2.1).

Table 2.1: Organisations within the Australian resources sector[11]

Tier	Market value	Number of organisations		
	$Billions (bn)	2012	2013	2014
Top	$5.00 and greater	8	7	10
Mid	$0.50 to $4.90	38	25	28
Low	$0.01 to $0.49	569	576	558

Organisational market value includes the construction cost of current projects with junior to mid-tier miners likely to be highly leveraged or seek scarce funds for their projects. In a globally competitive environment, organisations need to effectively meet adaptive challenges to capitalise on internally generated creativity and innovation and thus ensure the retention of this advantage within the organisation. Organisations also need new opportunities to create knowledge, cultures and behaviours that support adaptive outcomes, creativity and innovation to meet adaptive challenges.

The resources sector thrived before the onset of the GFC with its ramifications rippling through the business environment. However, in recent times, individuals have sought stability and security rather than transiency, whereas organisations have preferred to be lean and employ people on a contract or part-time basis. Thus, in the long term, employee tenure and loyalty provides limited assurance that individuals retain their status and roles within organisations.

The natural resources industry operates in challenging natural environments with temperatures above 35°C throughout the year, with minimal rainfall, and the occasional tropical cyclone which requires site evacuations. The sector relies on a fly-in, fly-out (FIFO) workforce, which requires back-to-back workers for the same roles, usually working on a 2:1 roster. A 2:1 roster operates over a three-week period during which workers stay onsite for 14-days in small, demountable buildings, colloquially known as 'dongas', and work 12-hour days followed by spending seven days at home on rest. The typical demographic of the workforce is blue-collar, low experience and male (90%). With regimented 12-hour working days and 14-day onsite rosters, organisations control individuals with long hours and high production demands, which makes site socialisation a challenge.

10. The Study Context

Some junior to mid-tier organisations within the natural resources sector operate as divisions of foreign-owned conglomerates commencing operations in greenfield investments. At different positions in their life cycles, these organisations have performed through traditional investment stages and currently operate at the production ramp-up stage.

Natural resources industries operate in distinct locations, involve significant investment in processes, due-diligence exploration, extraction, as well as construction and maintenance of related infrastructure.[1] Due to the complexity of extraction and refining processes, such industries usually comprise multiple structural nodes or process points and levels in organisational structures thus exhibiting traits of complex systems. For example, nodes can yield multiple interactions in and across different levels and have a network potential of deep, intense connections with strong coexisting bonds.[2] The strength of coexisting bonds results from the:

- quantity of time,
- the intensity of emotions,
- depth of relationship or intimacy and
- the exchange of support.[3]

To exploit available resources through employee heterogeneity, organisations that operate in complex environments require a degree of top-down, centralised control and bottom-up autonomy to innovate and respond effectively to dynamic global environments.[4] However, hierarchical and bureaucratic organisational structures impose limits on learning opportunities, knowledge creation and distribution, which influences innovation generation.[5] Conversely, innovative organisational structures comprise multidisciplinary groups which work with high degrees of freedom to facilitate cross-levels of knowledge.[6] Autonomy empowers the organisation to operate as an open rather than closed system and promotes information exchanges with and from the external mind.[7]

11. Innovation in the Resources Sector

A fundamental strategy to produce competitive advantage available to industries in the mature or saturation stage of their life cycle remains low-cost operations relative to other organisations in the same sector,[1] in addition to process innovation[2] to generate cost efficiencies.

Thus, given appropriate conditions in organisational environments, the possibility of creativity and process innovation exists at all points during the resource life cycle. However, the resources sector depends on the expertise and skills of knowledge workers, who keep abreast of new technologies and advancements in their fields. Therefore, knowledge workers can advise management on developments, which in the future may evolve into an organisation or industry-leading innovation.[3]

Two distinct characteristics of the resources sector determine the type of innovation the sector implements.[4] First, the resources sector has a relatively generic product, which means that continuous improvement of processes is more important than product innovation. Second, the resources sector generally uses tried and tested technology through acquired machinery and equipment with integrated innovation developed by other organisations. Thus, resource sector organisations tend to take minimal risks,[5] which limits innovation opportunities in the sector.

Figure 2.1 illustrates a typical mine life cycle curve, with the life cycle stages provided in Figure 2.2. Due to competition and specialities at different stages of the life cycle, there are possibilities for knowledge dissipation from organisations. Dissipation enables competitors to absorb knowledge and also generates opportunities for knowledge absorption.[6] Further, dissipation creates knowledge networks with the external mind that allow organisations to benefit from the exploration and implementation of innovative ideas undertaken by other organisations. However, a perception exists within some sectors of the resources industry that real change only occurs when organisations experience resource shortages. Thus, in newly established resource organisations, resource abundance restricts the scope of innovation in which creativity and innovation are nurtured predominantly as part of continuous improvement processes.

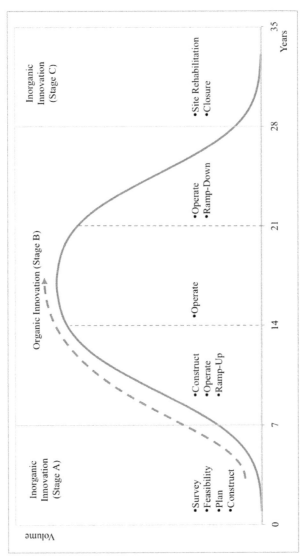

Figure 2.1: Mine life cycle curve[7]

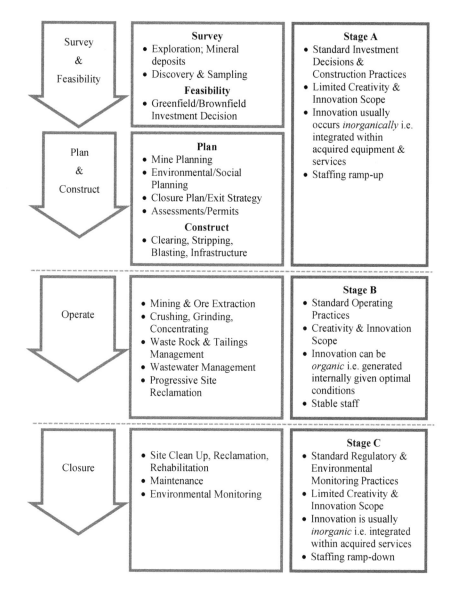

Survey & Feasibility	**Survey** • Exploration; Mineral deposits • Discovery & Sampling **Feasibility** • Greenfield/Brownfield Investment Decision	**Stage A** • Standard Investment Decisions & Construction Practices • Limited Creativity & Innovation Scope • Innovation usually occurs *inorganically* i.e. integrated within acquired equipment & services • Staffing ramp-up
Plan & Construct	**Plan** • Mine Planning • Environmental/Social Planning • Closure Plan/Exit Strategy • Assessments/Permits **Construct** • Clearing, Stripping, Blasting, Infrastructure	
Operate	• Mining & Ore Extraction • Crushing, Grinding, Concentrating • Waste Rock & Tailings Management • Wastewater Management • Progressive Site Reclamation	**Stage B** • Standard Operating Practices • Creativity & Innovation Scope • Innovation can be *organic* i.e. generated internally given optimal conditions • Stable staff
Closure	• Site Clean Up, Reclamation, Rehabilitation • Maintenance • Environmental Monitoring	**Stage C** • Standard Regulatory & Environmental Monitoring Practices • Limited Creativity & Innovation Scope • Innovation is usually *inorganic* i.e. integrated within acquired services • Staffing ramp-down

Figure 2.2: Mine life cycle stages[8]

As illustrated in Figure 2.1 and Figure 2.2, Stage A (the construction phase) usually involves limited innovation due to the construction, assembly and mobilisation of standard infrastructure. During this stage, innovation is predominantly inorganic and integrated with acquired equipment and services. Although resources sector organisations employ innovative ways to remain competitive, much of this innovation has been developed and implemented by external organisations or mind rather than through organic processes.[9] Thus, there has been a developing trend that encourages external mind engagement through the utilisation of contractors from other industries [10] which allows organisations to remain competitive and reduce costs. A product orientation may result in knowledge entrenchment in organisational products and internal processes, whereas some knowledge tacitly resides in its employees. Thus, product orientation increases the level of tacitness within organisations[11] and creates inherent risk transference to its customer base, adding pressure to the organisation to codify knowledge.

During Stage B, which reflects the productive years of the mine life cycle, innovation can be organic and internally generated. Due to competition from established markets such as South America and Canada, low-cost relativity and comparative advantage for resource organisations in Australia becomes critical. However, when organisations cannot be economical, they should vertically integrate their value chain to create a comparative advantage and thus guarantee product delivery.[12] Resource organisations are in a unique position to provide value-added raw material to international customers through vertically integrated value chains by utilising innovative processes that value-add to the extracted natural resource. Thus, resource organisations must engage in, generate and capitalise on organic creativity and innovation to maintain the competitive and comparative advantage. Capitalisation enables downstream, vertically linked industries to jointly share in the benefits of organically generated creativity and innovation efforts.[13]

Stage C reflects the end of mine-life during which organisations undertake rehabilitation and land reclamation projects. During this stage, standard regulatory and environmental procedures ensure no trace of activity remains. Therefore, during this stage, professional contractors provide specialist services and integrate creativity and innovation into the services they provide.

12. Chapter Summary

This chapter establishes the context for the study, provides an overview of the resources sector in Western Australia. It highlights and discusses different stages of the mine life cycle and the possibility of innovation. The importance of the resources industry to the Western Australian and global economy highlights the significance of encouraging innovation in the sector to maintain a competitive and comparative advantage over other organisations and countries.

Part Three: Cybernetic Leadership

Conservative views of leadership have a cybernetic focus in which leaders regulate and control organisational behaviour to achieve results through the use of feedback loops,[1] which constrains emergent self-organisation as an activity that requires management control.[2] Cybernetic leadership is traditionally attributed to position-based authority regardless of traits displayed within hierarchical positions, with conventional wisdom suggesting that leadership belongs to the person who occupies the position.[3]

A common perception also exists that cybernetic leadership involves an individual who exerts purposeful power over other individuals and directs them to achieve organisational goals.[4] However, cybernetic leadership fails to recognise that leadership can be embedded in complex interacting forces and does not merely occur through influential acts of single agents.[5]

Cybernetic leadership broadly includes two distinct styles of leadership: transactional or transformational,[6] which are usually present within the same organisation. The concern of transactional leaders is with routine processes such as resource distribution, and they observe and instruct their staff to achieve tasks in line with corporate objectives.[7] Whereas the concern of transformational leaders is with agential motivation, evolving concepts, and establishing a base for strategies, guidelines and processes[8] to foster creativity and innovation.[9]

Conversely, the cybernetic leadership model ensures compliance with organisational concepts and codified procedures that underlie homogeneity[10] and risk groupthink.

A critical view of the cybernetic leadership model claims that it makes inefficient usage of the creative potential and emotional commitment of employees.[11] Consequently, cybernetic leadership is less useful than adaptive leadership. Thus, some organisational leadership researchers suggest that leadership should evolve to consider more complex adaptive requirements and seek to value-add through social outcomes.[12]

13. Distribution

Many organisations exist in complex and dynamic environments that allow knowledge to increasingly fragment, which presents a challenge to identify, share and externalise knowledge.[1] The resources sector is such a dynamic environment where organisations mine, process and export homogenous natural resources at pre-agreed contractual quality tolerances. For organisations that offer such homogenous products, knowledge codification strategies to increase internal knowledge distribution and efficiencies are vital,[2] with knowledge clarified and documented in company policies, procedures, documents and job descriptions. The maintenance of such codified knowledge in predetermined and identified locations produces knowledge formalisation within organisational structures. However, sometimes codification can stifle innovation rather than find new solutions to challenges, so agents follow standard processes that result in tension.

Departments that pool and encourage knowledge distribution through organisational relationships assist and manage organisational complexity.[3] They ensure consistency and standardisation of processes, quality of products and allow for correction to predetermined tolerances. However, standardisation also results in initiative and creativity loss through the mechanical performance of functions in a pre-defined manner. The absence of dedicated departments as visible organisational symbols to encourage innovation results in reduced creativity and innovation. Symbols exist as significant features that agents can use to convey group assimilation, individuality, principles and philosophies.[4]

14. Functional Participation

Freely distributing and exchanging information in organisations creates a sense of camaraderie and ownership that can assist agents to uncover core values.[1] Thus, implicit knowledge distribution becomes a critical activity for organisational knowledge creation.[2] However, due to departmentalisation and homogeneity, organisations set up a limited array of functions and responsibilities, which restrict and narrow decision-making authority to assigned positions.[3]

Departmentalisation and homogeneity can dampen functional participation and creativity at lower levels because agents rely on instructions from other agents who control their actions. Prevalence of such behaviour, labelled as learned helplessness in organisations, causes agents to question why they should keep up with new ideas. However, curiosity, honesty and openness to new lessons increase judgement and consequently the quality of team output.

Resource organisations have separate processes and product streams, with value-add at each process node. Process separation and uniform products restrict and limit decision authority,[4] which consequently dampens creativity and innovation and results in organisational tension. Conversely, separation of individual roles and responsibilities create silos, which discourage the distribution of information and negatively influence knowledge opportunities.[5]

The opportunity for creativity and innovation exists at all organisational levels. Although, ideas mostly emerge from lower levels, which can allow culturally innovative organisations to implement and rapidly distribute innovations.[6] Agents at lower levels in organisations generate many ideas as they remain close to the action, and can identify opportunities and areas of improvement through associations and ideas to previously unidentified issues. Thus, agential contributions to organisational knowledge processes are more significant than hierarchy positions. Accordingly, organisations can introduce processes that support agents across all levels to present and discuss ideas to ensure creative contributions are non-hierarchical.

Functional participation involves self-development knowledge and development initiatives that agents generate[7] in addition to creative solutions that agents implement without prior approval because they recognise a need. Consequently, self-development support without constraints or conditions of tuition reimbursement can be beneficial as agents can apply the training to increase task diversity. Task diversity also allows functional participation to transpire because of agential availability to assist and interact. Much staff development also occurs on the job; therefore it is essential to provide support to agents who pursue self-development initiatives.

15. Enabling Leadership

Organisations require leadership to generate and set the direction[1] for knowledge creation, distribution and retention. Enabling leadership structures and facilitates conditions that encourage creativity, problem-solving, learning and increased adaptability within organisations.[2] Enabling leadership also facilitates complex functions at a formal level to enact adaptive leadership in informal networks within organisations. Further, adaptive leadership injects tension to stimulate interactions and generates interdependencies among organisational agents.[3] Leadership attributes identified through the case study, which facilitate structure and enable conditions that allow for creativity and innovation to flourish in organisations, align with an enabling leadership approach. These attributes are further explored and discussed in this Part.

16. Workers

Knowledge workers possess the necessary skills, experience and competence to make them efficient and complement skillsets to allow teams to effectively function. Knowledge workers quickly determine specific requirements for particular instances through the associations they create with prior experiences. Thus, organisational workers have effectively become apprentices with innate abilities to move around and find multiple job opportunities based on the skills and qualifications they possess.[1] On the part of the worker, knowledge work demands continuous up-skilling as well as access to opportunities to practice [2] as the worker can choose where they work.[3]

In recent resource boom times, labour shortages occurred as a significant issue, which resulted in the inability of labour to be transient. Despite a reduction of opportunities for workers with crucial skills, the problem of transiency remains pertinent. Teamwork in organisations is critical for knowledge creation because agents in teams continually interact and reflect on the diverse meanings drawn by other individuals. A reflection on the diversity of meanings challenges agents to reassess ambiguous meanings that then result in new knowledge.[4] Reassessing ambiguous meanings allows for the development of rich connections to increase the possibility of several viewpoints that strengthen intelligence and foster self-organisation.[5]

Organisational environments also socially construct and deconstruct with the formation of each connection, which allows the organisation to analyse and dynamically address any new information.[6] In multicultural organisations, diversity and tension between non-Western and Western management ideologies challenge the cross-cultural creation and nurture of rich connections with information withheld or restricted to members of respective silos.

17. Consult and Engage

Organisations can maximise their operational success when agents engage, consult with peers and seek advice to share responsibilities for issues.[1] Consultation with peers also allows managers to proactively handle challenges and seek input from all levels within the organisation.[2] Conversely, a lack of peer consultation in organisations results in agents acting without reference to management despite decisions affecting all levels. Increased peer consultation can proactively prevent issues and enhance awareness to facilitate informed decisions that benefit the organisation.

Agents on the front line of customer service or production usually carry the most organisational intellectual capital because they understand customers' product requirements. However, these agents may lack appreciation, as management ignore their views.[3] Thus, agents must feel appreciated for their knowledge pool contribution before they will engage in knowledge and value creation activities.[4] Knowledge and value creation activities can become challenging if agents at lower organisational levels are without support. Organisations, therefore, need to identify ways to engage agents at all levels to influence functional participation. Agential belief systems also manifest as their 'basin of attraction, and a point of stability', i.e. the mental or physical structure or space towards which agential behaviours gravitate to in times of uncertainty and instability. Such 'basins of attraction,' interchangeably referred to as 'attractor pits' or 'attractor basins' allow individuals to make sense of uncertainty and instability in the process resonating and facilitating new interconnections, behaviours, or the emergence of new problems. [5]

Leadership requires additional energy to dislodge such belief systems to facilitate the convergence of agential points of stability to a new basin of attraction[6] and to allow different patterns of interaction to strengthen.[7] Thus, corporate training must encourage, engage and provide agents with guidance for solutions to organisational challenges, as well as encourage agential functional participation. Functional participation assists in the career progression of agents, supports knowledge retention and encourages knowledge distribution in the organisation. Agents also achieve engagement that permits cover for when other agents happen to be away.

The use of external contractors as a transient employee strategy is risky because contractors may use open positions to get employed and then seek other opportunities after they have some job security. With contractors only around for short periods, this results in departmental knowledge leakage and discontinuity. However, in some instances, due to the nature of the work and contractors' areas of expertise, organisations can choose to engage skilled contractors and consultants on a temporary basis.

18. Taken for Granted

Individuals seldom work hard in the current moment for future compensation.[1] Organisations need to, therefore, provide ongoing rewards and recognition to motivate and encourage productivity. Psychological contracts inherent in relationships between organisations and agents create expectations based on implicit or explicit expectations in promises or mutual commitments.[2] An organisational expectation also exists that agents improve their roles continuously without any recognition or reward for their efforts. A breach of implied expectations naturally occurs when organisations take agents for granted. Time control of onsite agents can also result when organisations command and take agents for granted. There is an urgent need for boundaries between organisational activities and social activities. Among 42 findings in the Education and Health Standing Committee study, a current debate in the study of FIFO work arrangements in the Western Australian resources sector agrees and additionally highlights the control of accommodation facilities as a mental health risk factor. The study reports:

"Accommodation facilities for FIFO workers are often self-contained, highly regulated, and subject to considerable control

measures. It is not clear that all control measures are required for worker health and safety. The Committee questions whether such high levels of control when workers are off shift and in the accommodation facilities are necessary.[3] "

Work engagement relates to external factors such as changes in personal or social circumstances of individuals', which affect stimulation or motivation.[4] Work engagement mediates between empowerment and change,[5] with empowerment seen as a motivational concept.[6] Further, a gap in the current research literature exists that links innovation in organisations to organisational attitudes and psychological processes.[7]

Agents within organisations also face the choice of whether to speak up or remain silent when they have ideas, concerns, or useful information. Agential voicing of concerns prevails as a gap in current academic research.[8] Psychological contracts in some organisations dictate that the ability to recognise and fix organisational issues remains a part of agential roles without expectation of reward or acknowledgement. While some individuals appreciate intangible recognition for improvements, others expect physical rewards which then creates tension or conflict because some individuals require a tangible reward to voice ideas, the lack of which results in voice suppression. Occasionally, agents may also mechanically execute management direction, lack initiative to improve their roles and thereby take their own position roles for granted. Consequently, tension exists when organisations see creativity and innovation as role-centric. Further, agents may perceive creativity and innovation as secondary and, therefore, lack initiative.

19. Empowerment

Empowering agents to take on increased challenges and become multi-skilled provides them with different perspectives as well as the ability to analyse issues. However, when organisations become too prescriptive, agents do not take ownership of challenges. Consequently, agents need authority as well as the responsibility to be creative and determine better ways to complete tasks. An agential awareness of industrial innovation assists organisations to analyse and understand the solutions that other organisations develop and execute. Through empowerment, agents can also identify problems, solve issues and confidently present innovative solutions that organisations can implement.

Creativity can be vision-driven or management and organisational goals guided.[1] Accordingly, organisations can allow explicit goals and directives to guide agents, solve adaptive challenges and achieve creativity. Through consultation processes, agential flexibility can increase and identify potential solutions, thereby circumventing organisational objections on solutions that foster creativity. Clear communications of agential goal ownership can also aid and improve processes.

Organic cultural aspects affect intrinsic agential motivations to engage in creative and innovative behaviour. Issues such as a lack of emotional awareness or intimidation on the part of management demotivate agents and results in reactive rather than proactive responses from them. Perceived power assumptions result in withheld codified tacit knowledge, which causes demotivation. Wasted effort and resources also result from data that are held on local storage on individual computers rather than shared publicly on a network, which exercises power over others, with other agents unaware of the existence of valuable information.

20. Respect

Within a complex system environment, open and honest conversations are a critical source and energy conduit that allows the system to function and brings distributed intelligence into play.[1] Respect and integrity towards agents in organisations are crucial to foster relationships. Consequently, organisations should treat agents with respect to promote interactions and honest, open conversations.

Creativity remains the responsibility of each agent and is critical at all organisational levels.[2] Creativity results from the identification of methods to modify or create new approaches to undertake organisational tasks, whereas innovation results from the implementation of these new processes.[3] To be deemed as creative responses, products need to be:

- original,
- relevant,

- beneficial and
- accurate or essential for exploratory rather than rational tasks.

Additionally, 'a product or response will be judged as creative to the extent that (a) it is both a novel and appropriate, useful, correct, or valuable response to the task at hand and (b) the task is heuristic rather than algorithmic'.[4]

Regardless of their origin, all ideas require due consideration for their value to the organisation, where value consideration demonstrates respect for agents who generate and present creative or innovative ideas. However, some organisations have hierarchical structures that hinder creativity, which creates tension between the need to recognise ideas from across all levels and a structure that discounts these ideas. Current resources can also generate novel ideas or products and contain newer elements resulting in concepts or products that previously did not exist.[5] Innovation will remain an extension of a current product or process, or as part of a continuous improvement process with creativity and innovation as a mechanism for it. As a result, change in many organisations will likely be novel. Internal and external networks of skilled and talented individuals who engage and challenge current products and processes to make them better remain at the core of global innovation.

Creativity results from people who encourage and inspire other agents to think independently and be creative, thus teamwork fosters creativity through working innovatively smart work. However, management acceptance of solutions remains an issue in many organisations because most innovation is incrementally generated and has limited reach.[6] The application of continuous improvement processes makes agents creative, effective and efficient, which aims to achieve progressive performance improvements through gradual but constant change that focuses on increasing organisational effectiveness and efficiency to fulfil objectives.[7]

The need for motivated staff and other factors that determine motivation emerge from the case study and include the right people for the job and those who thrive on continuous improvement in a context in which organisations expect, but do not reward, creativity and innovation. However, due to cultural or operational issues, some parts of the case study may not work together, and some agents may attempt to correct problems without due diligence or necessary work approvals, which could result in sub-optimal solutions.

Innovation and creativity are crucial to organisational success.[8] Accordingly, voluntary exits from organisations can arise when teams in organisations become dormant and demotivated through a lack of respect from upper management which can have the consequence of accumulated corporate intelligence leakage. Alternatively, agents might stay in the organisation but do not contribute to continuous improvement or change initiatives.

Reflexivity is a process through which individuals interpret their thoughts and opinions, assess their circumstances and support, make choices and establish projects based on their interests. [9] Reflexivity fosters awareness towards organisational objectives, strategies and the environment among agents and aligns with innovation challenges.[10] Thus, reflexivity promotes team productivity and innovation. However, the case study suggests that scope for greater reflexivity on the part of management may exist, particularly in the display of respect for those who initiate productive changes. It also appears that when managers take credit for other people's efforts, creativity is constrained or dampened.

Intolerance for ambiguity due to strategic gaps[11] or a lack of respect from management stifles functional participation and results in agential incapacity to persist in creative endeavours. Thus, lack of vision from senior management or their inability to communicate this vision can also stifle agential functional participation.

Appreciation, recognition, respect and reward for agential effort motivates, promotes and drives creativity and innovation, which results in an increased commitment to organisational goals.[12] However, psychological contracts dictate that creativity and innovation occur because of normal day-to-day operations and are part of agential roles with the lack of necessary award or recognition. Thus, as a means to motivate people to be creative and innovative, organisations require a **formal reward, recognition or bonus structure** which links to performance. A rewards structure, however, needs careful consideration and design, which can range from bonuses and promotions to job retention and simple acknowledgement of a job well done.

21. Right People

Although only practical with readily available talent, organisations can use the process of knowledge acquisition to replace or buy in new talent. Knowledge acquisition can increase competency through integration.[1] In the case of a skills shortage, however, this is a risky proposition because acquired knowledge may be costly, might not be the right knowledge or at the desired levels of competence. Organisational management can facilitate relationships among agents to coordinate the right people to capitalise on strategic gaps[2] that long-serving agents make easy as they possess more comprehensive experience and capabilities, which the organisation can then realise. Although, in some cases, it remains efficient and economical for organisations to outsource projects to the external mind.

When managers recruit people with appropriate skills, information sharing processes, feedback, understanding and identification of opportunities become easier.[3] Additionally, recruitment becomes more manageable and ensures the right fit with previous knowledge of incumbents' capabilities. Conversely, performance management of inappropriate agents can become an arduous process which demotivates the whole team. In the case study, the inadequacy of the organisation's probation arose due to insufficient pre-employment due diligence as candidates sometimes pretended to fit in just for the duration of their probation period. Thus, managers need to recruit the right people whose values fit with organisational values.[4]

Due diligence to select the right candidate remains an urgent issue with 'fair and transparent' and 'ethical' being the two concerns of the HR departments in the recruitment and selection process.[5] The placement of untested agents in senior positions remains a problem that compromise HR departments and dampen creativity and innovation, which makes promotion and progression unlikely. Conversely, organisations can assign the right people in the most important roles to have a competitive advantage and survive.[6]

People with the right skills survive as high performers who encourage and motivate their peers to perform at higher standards. Although, people born between the years 1965–1980 (Generation X) prefer to follow the lead of experienced peers, seek out and implement the best innovative ideas and value clear organisational strategies linked to a direction.[7] With no dedicated resources to promote creativity and innovation in organisational structures, even with the right people, creativity and innovation will not develop. Therefore, to foster creativity and innovation, organisations need to consider these requirements in the development of their recruitment strategies.

Organisations need to develop an environment of trust through internal processes which stimulates innovation, leads to a raised emotional stability, facilitates the acceptance and openness of expression and encourages agential risk-taking.[8] Management trust and confidence are prerequisites for effective knowledge management within organisations.[9] The acts of management have a significant influence on the development of a culture of trust because their cumulative actions help determine internal climate. For example, the impositions of dramatic control hierarchies or subversions of capable team members show disrespect for individuals and erode trust,[10] which results in demotivation and reluctance to cooperate and share knowledge. When managers share control with employees, it demonstrates the assurance that the employees have the required motivation and skills. Further, trust increases employees' commitment and ultimately retains knowledge.[11]

With trusted agents in organisations, interaction, discussion of ideas and knowledge distribution become easier.[12] Conversely, a lack of trust ensues when individuals take credit for the work of other individuals, which results in withheld knowledge. Trust builds in management when organisations communicate and regularly let people know about corporate developments. The time spent in the company of other agents also results in a higher degree of trust among agents.[13] The advantage of time spent together highlights the benefits of after-work functions, which build rapport and trust.

22. Team

Complexity leadership recognises the benefits of team composition flexibility, which determines interactions through the self-governing entry and exit of agents independently from organisational leaders.[1]

However, some organisations also have teams that operate and perform well outside of preferred complexity leadership patterns. For example, in FIFO environments, some teams function well but are controlled by management and most workers have little discretion available to them.

Resident diverse knowledge and skills through agential role splits can help organisations achieve common goals by organisationally distributing knowledge and injecting energy.[2] Well-functioning teams provide greater efficiencies and productivity returns as individual strengths complement and negate weaknesses through interactions that enable team members to build stronger personal relationships. Results from this case study indicate that agents with multiple skills foster creativity and innovation as a knowledge distribution activity, which is salient to the organisation because operational roles and roles that affect production remain critical to the continuity and functioning of the organisation. Thus, agents with multiple skills can assist and reduce recruitment and training costs.[3] Organisations should therefore create opportunities between different departments for ideas to cross-pollinate which lead to an increase in social capital and knowledge transfer.[4] Facilitating staff movement at departmental and organisational levels also increases agential interactions and the distribution of knowledge, which can lead to cross-pollination and a better overview of operations.

Organisations exist as being either low or high care.[5] In low-care organisations codified knowledge predominantly exists as explicit i.e. documented processes, with sharing occurring on a transactional basis because organisations limit social interaction and restrict the distribution of tacit knowledge. Conversely, high-care organisations encourage social interactions and intrinsically facilitate tacit knowledge distribution.[6] Relationships in high-care organisations exist with higher value and degree of care among agents, which makes agents highly accessible and lenient, with a greater inclination to help colleagues.[7] On the other hand, low-care organisations rely on documented standard policies and operational procedures, with interactions among amenable agents. Thus, multinational organisations often suffer from increased administration and standardisation, which decreases initiative and increases rigidity.[8]

Knowledge distribution and retention through job rotation programs and a knowledgeable network allow agents to learn and understand organisational roles, as well as providing the motivation to encourage employee development and ensure adequate leave cover. Job rotation signifies a risky proposition as the existence of tacit knowledge between agents can result in knowledge leakage.[9] However, job rotation within multinational organisations increases interactions between staff from diverse cultures and backgrounds,[10] thus bringing in varied perspectives to organisational challenges. On balance, job rotation can be beneficial to multicultural organisations because it increases interactions among different cultures. Organisations should carefully implement these programs to ensure agents can equally contribute and learn from others.

23. Tenure

Agential turnover can result from various factors which include a lack of mutual integration, conflict and disagreement, as well as incompetence. Turnover has an inverse relationship to tenure in that an increase in tenure results in turnover reduction.[1] Increase in tenure initially enhances skills and performance, which ultimately peaks then declines, and results in diminishing creativity, motivation and innovation.[2] Long-tenured knowledgeable employees may, however, be sceptical and conditioned to respond slowly to challenges through learned helplessness.[3] Redundancies and removal of agents from the organisation who do not perform also affect tenure.[4] Consequently, sector volatility means that most agents have either directly or indirectly been part of a redundancy.

24. Operationalising

This case study engages two objectives:

1. Investigate how adaptive leadership operationalises in the resource sector.
2. Explore how creativity and innovation generate internally from informal agential interaction.

These two objectives associate through data, which reveals elements of adaptive leadership that remain present in the case study organisation but these elements exist alongside other practices that more closely align with cybernetic leadership. Fully operationalising adaptive leadership by management within organisations remains incomplete. Despite this, perceptions of factors that hinder or foster creativity and innovation provide insight into current organisational practices which facilitate and limit the extent to which informal agential interaction can generate creativity and innovation.

Understanding agential composition helps organisations recognise human capital dynamics, knowledge creation, distribution, withholds, retention and relationships between agents, and dispersion within teams. Knowledge retention can take a long time to reap the benefits of cumulative tacit knowledge and training investments.[1] Effective management of knowledge creation and retention is crucial for competitive and comparative advantage for organisations.[2] Thus, organisations should build agential commitment, engage their emotional energy and attention[3] and allow meaningful relationships with each other to share knowledge and prevent leakage.

Knowledge creation and codification occur through effective knowledge distribution, adequate training, organisational openness and multi-skilled agents, alongside a commitment that, 'all ideas and concepts should be viewed and not just tossed out.' Further, a specialist versus generalist view of human capital within organisations identifies specialists with field-specific knowledge, whereas generalists possess a variety of skills.[4]

Because generalists have multiple skills, organisations can deploy them to a variety of areas. Generalists contrast with a large proportion of onsite staff who tend to be specialist in nature; for example, agents require a specific licence and experience to operate dump trucks onsite or specialist training to maintain the dump trucks that can each be worth more than $7 million.

Organisations can foster commitment, appeal to the passion and devotion of agents and engage them to relate and feel a sense of pride about the organisation and group.[5] As part of a knowledge creation and distribution strategy, job rotation and cross-training enables departments to function and provide services to their stakeholders even while staff members are away or on training courses.

In organisations, an incorrect assumption of free information flows exist where the use of readily available technologies means that agents often withhold and treat raw, processed data and knowledge information as a valuable commodity.[6] Consistent with this view, findings from this case study indicate that at an organisational level, some managers remain reluctant to share information. Some agents at lower levels also view knowledge as a source of power and create a silo mentality within the organisation.

As a counter to knowledge silos, differences between a full-time and transient individual can become parallel to and dovetail with other agents, which ensures organisations have an informed network that allows adequate knowledge retention within it to operate effectively on a day-to-day basis. The relationship between dovetail and parallel occurs as an optimal relationship between responsibility and authority over knowledge within the organisation.[7] Consequently, transient employees should work closely together to ensure awareness of current uncompleted tasks within their teams. Most positions in resource organisations are FIFO, which requires back-to-back systems in which two agents perform tasks but at different ends of their FIFO roster. In such an arrangement, one individual takes a break and the other individual works the role, therefore dovetail and parallel become crucial to maintaining continuity.

One of the possible adverse consequences of a natural resources economy is the reallocation of production away from other industrial sectors.[8] Consequently, this only occurs within a commodity boom cycle, with a reversal of effects during a commodity bust. Due to commodity price volatility, employees who have minimal knowledge and experience within the industry are the first to become redundant.[9] Thus, the cyclical boom and bust nature of the sector, which usually has a finite resource life introduces complexity in the recruitment needs within the mine life cycle. Figure 2.2 illustrates how the requirement to recruit staff increases in Stage A with ramp-up activities. Stage B has a stable labour requirement with a steady rate of production while in Stage C, the labour requirement decreases with ramp-down activities. Labour requirements have consequences as shortages exist in a boom cycle, whereas excesses exist during bust cycles. Therefore, organisations have to restructure to remain cost-competitive, which can result in an organisation's inability to capitalise on creativity and innovation or retain knowledge.

When organisations restructure and downsize their operations, they may depreciate their intellectual capital, which results in the deterioration of intellectual capital.[10] Restructures and redundancies are knowledge retention barriers for organisations, with knowledge loss that demotivates and makes agents withdraw.

In economic downturns or redundancies, as a result of their shared experiences, agents left in organisations tend to unite and feel closer to each other.[11] Organisations in which demands and loyalties conflict in economic downturns, this does not necessarily happen, thereby affecting knowledge distribution and retention. In such times, people management remains challenging as it involves the selection of the type and level of knowledge that organisations try and retain. Conversely, the welfare of agents made redundant remains equally important, which makes guiding teams difficult and results in diminished knowledge distribution. Therefore, decisions on which organisational knowledge to lose or retain become challenging due to the possibility for tacit knowledge loss.

In periods of redundancies, less staff creates increased workload stress for those who survive, which disrupts positivity within the organisation and can lead to concerns over job security, in the process causing further distress and demotivating staff. Employees who survive restructures within organisations fear job retention, which also results in dampened creativity and innovation. Due to the dynamic nature of the resources sector, agents seek job security and stability through reduced voluntary change. Reduction in the voluntary movement was particularly evident after the GFC when job security became increasingly important.[12]

As an alternative concept to making staff redundant, organisations can instead create repetitive capacity or recurrency.[13] In this context, redundancy relates to the distribution of intelligence, which allows data to be widely available and causes agents to become self-aware and system aware. Such organisations have widely distributed intelligence networks that tend to exhibit redundancy at many levels.[14] Network redundancy results in multi-source inputs thus, interference in one input does not interrupt the complete system but instead strengthens the already complex and robust network.[15] Network redundancy creates repeated processes,[16] facilitates tacit knowledge transfer and supports newly generated explicit knowledge distribution.[17] Further, cross-training or strategic rotation also assist in recurrency because they allow agents to understand the business from different angles and input sources, which facilitates the smooth transfer and flow of organisational knowledge. However, rather than use cross-training to foster creativity and innovation, organisations explicitly and deliberately undertake to cross-train as a knowledge distribution activity.

Some tension appears when managers utilise a 'mission command' philosophy. Mission command advocates authority and control to arrive at an end state as agents see fit. However, when agents follow a pre-identified codified method, this conflicts with ownership to arrive at an end state. Standard laid down processes effectively stifle creative thought and create stress between processes that aim to ensure conformity against a philosophy of freedom to achieve an end state. Thus, as an essential condition, tension stimulates interactions and generates interdependencies among organisational agents to enact adaptive leadership.[18]

A mission command philosophy asserts on the premise that gives agents freedom and initiative, to increase decision-making when preparation in operations becomes difficult and uncertain.[19] Mission command also increases flexibility to deal with unforeseen events, delegates accountability and stimulates creativity throughout the organisation.[20]

Standard procedures and operational processes facilitate the retention of collective corporate intelligence, with the main task of managers seen to increase connectivity among agents, and in the process, enhance cooperation and knowledge.[21] Collective corporate intelligence can occur during meetings, workshops and platforms to brainstorm, share and interact. Thus, organisations can brainstorm to generate ideas[22] or solutions to current challenges. However, the initiation of brainstorm sessions that assists agents to codify and subsequently improve processes remains difficult. Brainstorm sessions occur as further inclusive views of issues on hand, as managers recognise intended solutions but need to know that they have considered everything in the process.

Activities designed to deliver new ideas through processes such as brainstorms appear to have an opposite force when managers instinctively guide solutions that conflict with the usage of these activities. This process, known as coaching, occurs when managers intuitively establish desired results to influence the behaviour of agents and the delivery of outcomes.[23] Interactions and meetings also occur as forms of brainstorms and a means to increase connectivity among agents.

Organisations use open-innovation processes to interact externally to procure or advance ideas.[24] The use of consultants to conduct specific projects can be an open-innovation activity because it allows organisations to acquire external ideas. However, agents view consultants negatively and suspiciously as people who use the organisation as a means to penetrate the sector, which can affect creativity and innovation opportunities.

IP (Intellectual Property) for work consultants generate in some organisations may belong to the consultants and can therefore create a knowledge retention risk. Consequently, external knowledge stores become non-exclusive, easily acquired and widely available to competitors. Loss of control risk also exists for the organisation when competitors exploit this knowledge.[25] As a result, tension exists when organisations engage consultants to support open innovation and the loss of competitive advantage through possible knowledge loss with competitors.

When organisations adapt knowledge retention strategies, they face 'integrate-or-relate' dilemmas, with the prospect of internal integration of the knowledge they acquire or reliance on consultants as the external mode of knowledge retention.[26] However, there is currently a lack of research on knowledge retention that deals with knowledge leakage which occurs when long-tenured knowledge workers leave organisations.[27] A reliance on transient social capital has implications for organisations with the integrate-or-relate and leakage of knowledge dilemmas, which results in an adverse effect on the internal capitalisation of creativity and innovation.

25. Encouragement

Knowledge continuity hinges on honesty, openness, feedback and a culture of innovation.[1] Whereas some managers actively encourage innovative activities, others do not have any explicit means for this process. Formal performance measures for agents to learn aspects of different areas of the organisation can inspire agents to participate functionally and facilitate the creation of social capital. Functional participation results in and contributes to structural capital creation within organisations.[2]

Supportive social and emotional spaces are essential to increase engagement[3] with problem delegation, which also allows people to work on problems to facilitate new solutions and foster knowledge and creativity. Thus, organisations should identify agential potential and provide challenges for such agents to encourage performance at a higher level. Managers should also understand how to foster and enable an engagement culture rather than attempt to coerce it.[4] Although, creativity and innovation depend on agents who naturally perform at a high level regardless of encouragement, and without transparent processes in place to escalate ideas it remains an agential responsibility to promote ideas to management. The lack of transparent processes can result in stress because some organisation structures may not encourage innovation, thus the implementation of an open process to evaluate new ideas will help foster innovation.

26. Fear

Fear stifles creativity and innovation and can manifest in different ways, including fear of failure,[1] fear of assumptions and performance questions, fear of empowerment or fear to make decisions.[2] These fears are more pronounced in high-power distance cultures where agents expect direction[3] and in Eastern cultures in which fear of face loss applies,[4] and can adversely affect initiative.[5] Foreign organisations experience significant challenges to establish operations in other countries, which often compound into budget overruns and create a culture of fear and face loss. Consequently, the certainty of global competition demands a corporate growth focus rather than a focus on retrenchments and reducing costs.[6] When organisations focus on size and cost reduction, they create a climate of fear and dampen creativity and innovation.

Fear and control linked to motivation correlate with leadership behaviours generally accepted within organisations. For example, fear and control affect intrinsic motivation and can relate to a style of leadership that seeks to control activities to have predictable outcomes. Managers can also suppress innovative ideas within organisations, which causes restricted and hindered knowledge flows due to their behaviour and complacency or the reluctance of agents to get involved. Restructures and redundancies also create environments of organisational knowledge leakage which can be involuntary, a result of restructures and redundancies, or voluntary when agents leave for personal reasons. Thus, knowledge leakage can result in staff demotivation and learned helplessness.

High staff turnover creates a significant loss of tacit awareness, which makes personnel retention and organisational knowledge important. As evident from rash redundancies during economic downturns, as well as the voluntary movement of agents between organisations within the sector, organisations seldom give enough thought to which individuals and what knowledge to retain resulting in a lack of loyalty within the resources sector. Knowledge retention is critical to ensure agents that remain after redundancies understand organisational systems and processes and safeguard organisational continuity.

Redundancies demotivate and impact morale with adverse effects on organisational performance. Although redundancies affect team dynamics and interactions, during downturns organisations have to be realistic and reduce labour expenditure. Tacit knowledge leakage also occurs when agents leave the organisation through their own accord. Additionally, extended leave periods such as sick leave or maternity leave create conditions for specific tacit knowledge leakage when agents do not resume their roles, and results in agential pressure and disruption as continuity of service can sometimes result in the employment of unsuitable contractors.

Organisations sometimes do not consider staffing suitably and make positions redundant, which affects knowledge retention due to a lack of essential resources for task completion. However, when organisations facilitate interactions among agents, organisations can build rapport, trust and cooperation among agents and across departments, and can break down mentality and cultural silos.

Senior managers may use fear to support their decisions and create unease or tension within their areas of responsibility, which instils a culture of withholding information and results in unforeseen issues. Due to the prevalence of redundancies and restructures in the sector, being a permanent employee provides a false sense of security because organisations can let employees go at any time, making all employees non-permanent or temporary.

27. Openness

Openness is required to create cultural change and inspire agents to share and codify tacit knowledge throughout organisations.[1] Open communication to address the importance of challenges faced by organisations can foster functional participation and allow agents to appreciate the effects on each team member. However, demanding workloads require agents to focus on critical activities, which hinders their creative efforts, thus it is essential to encourage employees to focus on an organisational theme or overarching vision.[2] Further, openness allows organisations to analyse issues productively to foster creativity and innovation.

Conversely, agents may communicate regularly but still withhold information or ideas about their awareness of organisational challenges if they believe management will reject their ideas,[3] which results in both the withholding of knowledge as well as the fear of expressing contrary views. Creativity and innovation can nurture when agents clearly understand the expectations of them, although agents may hold certain beliefs that encourage silence and actively suppresses their views within organisations.[4] Resulting from these belief systems, employees frequently confront voice dilemmas and concerns to express their creative thoughts.[5] Thus, management should continuously work to dispel these beliefs, encourage and reward agential voice to foster openness associated with conditions that facilitate creativity and innovation.

28. Process

The innate nature of knowledge leakage necessitates organisation-wide tacit knowledge and skills distribution through a codification and transfer process.[1] Codification results in knowledge that organisations save for later retrieval and application, aiming to formalise knowledge through capture, make knowledge explicit and represent it in understandable formats.[2] Among other methods, codification involves the documentation of how employees perform and complete their duties. In the process, organisations maintain various electronic corporate databases that contain detailed transactional data to analyse their operations, as well as to develop appropriate competitive strategies.

Internal processes and routines include tacit organisational rules and procedures, which determine workflow and the distribution of these rules and procedures throughout organisations.[3] Knowledge transfer consequently occurs through a process that organisations use to make agents aware of the routines and practices.[4] Prevalent organisational cultures shape the processes that assist in the creation and adoption of knowledge within organisations.[5]

Agents also expect updated information that makes it the responsibility of each area to ensure this creatively occurs. In some instances, codified procedures exist for non-complex work due to a need to follow processes that assure work consistency. However, codified procedures can result in tension between rigidly standardised manners to perform responsibilities against the flexibility required to ensure agents think creatively about task completion. A rigid standardised process can result in stagnation due to mechanical completion of tasks.

29. Structure

Organisational structures can be different; however, most start-up organisations use sectoral best practice as a model. Best practice can assist organisations in recognising how they should operate as well as identify the risks and opportunities they will encounter. Start-up organisations have ambitious ideas, the agility of action, can take risks and have a vision of growth for the organisation. Due to this initial setup, start-up organisations can be innovative.[1] At the design or feasibility stage, innovation remains possible (see Stage A in Figure 2.1: "Mine life cycle curve" and Stage A in Figure 2.2: "Mine life cycle stages") Although, if an organisation misses this opportunity, it effectively locks into a design methodology until the project finally commissions. Organisations require better roles and responsibilities structure with less hierarchical levels as well as communication because an absence of teamwork can result in a silo mentality. Such structures facilitate interactions and discussion across the hierarchy to increase opportunities to foster creativity and innovation.

Part Four: Intellectual Capital

Enveloped within an adaptive leadership framework in an organic context, three main groups of factors influence creativity and innovation. In this case study, these predominantly reflect individual, relational or organisational factors. However, these characteristics link, overlap and influence each other in intricate ways through the tension that makes distinct compartmentalisation of characteristic impractical. This next section begins with a description of these characteristics.

30. Individual Characteristics

Much of the academic literature and research focuses on specific properties of agents and the importance of these for organisational creativity and innovation,[1] including how these characteristics interact and relate with other agents within organisations. Individually treated, these properties reside in and remain integral to the behaviour and conduct of organisational agents. Broadly grouped into intellectual capital, human capital and social capital, individual characteristics follow in detail below.

Social capital identifies as the resource that entrenches in and is accessible through, agential relationship networks.[2] Social capital fosters human capital,[3] which consists of the **knowledge, skills and abilities that agents take with them when they leave an organisation.**[4] Consequently, as collective knowledge, intellectual capital resides in organisational human capital. Numerous academic researchers have discussed and described the concept of intellectual capital.[5] However, these researchers are yet to identify a universally accepted definition.[6] Intellectual capital are inclusive organisational abilities, experiences, cultures, strategies, processes, intellectual property and relational networks which create competitive value and comparative advantage to help organisations realise their goals.[7]

Recognised as assets and commonly categorised into the organisational, human, relational and structural capital,[8] intellectual capital underpins organisational capabilities and core competencies and performs a pivotal strategic role[9] in sustainability.

Collectively referred to as intellectual capital, intangibles can generate corporate value[10] and occur as unrecognised assets and undisclosed resources, elements or capacities that facilitate organisational strategy.[11] Thus, intellectual capital remains a resource vital for the survival of an organisation and its ability to be innovative and significantly maps the way organisations perform, succeed[12] and drive growth and competitive position in markets.

Tacit knowledge resident in intellectual capital is crucial for commercial power generation,[13] competitive advantage and sustainability. Tacit knowledge comprises of **agential insights and approaches that differentiate experts from non-skilled workers and often allow agents to make sense of and understand their knowledge gaps.**

Sustainable change necessitates a combination and essential transformation at three levels:

- mental,
- emotional and
- spiritual.[14]

Rather than a religious context or an Eastern philosophy, the spiritual level here refers to a need that provides reflection, importance and significance to agents as well as organisations. Thus, creativity develops at a spiritual level and makes creative and quantum thought processes comparable.[15] Intellectual capital also refers to knowledge and the capability to understand social collectives.[16] Therefore, to develop adequate intellectual capital, groups must cultivate and foster at mental, emotional and spiritual levels.

Intellectual capital can result from creativity or knowledge, which ultimately converts into innovation.[17] Further, social capital comprises of structural, relational and cognitive dimensions, which facilitate the creation of new intellectual capital. New intellectual capital emerges through agential interaction and allows sharing of information and knowledge by the development of trust, shared norms, obligations and identity.[18]

Due to the urgent need to convert data into useful information in uncertain and turbulent environments, organisations need to learn to survive. As an organisational core competency, constructive development of social capital is one of the problems that leaders face to retain intellectual capital.[19] Social capital development generates and shares tacit organisational knowledge[20] to take advantage of new opportunities.[21] Consequently, a principal source for competitive advantage remains talent that excels, which is why organisations that seek to make effective use of competitive advantage must introduce a talent mindset because 'superior talent' remains a prime source of competitive advantage. Companies seeking to exploit competitive advantage must, therefore, instil a talent mindset throughout the organisation.[22]

In the medium-term or long-term, innovation remains the only reliable means for organisations to create and achieve high-quality results.[23] In which, the transfer of information or knowledge occurs through interconnected agents,[24] whom organisations value as knowledge workers.[25] Thus, to exploit knowledge internally, organisations should expose agents to opportunities that facilitate external knowledge acquisition and encourage internalisation through interaction and communication. Internal knowledge exploitation further develops agential and organisational knowledge. Employment security can also generate and maintain social capital, therefore, remuneration strategies that reward teams and agents who give prominence to teamwork will cultivate interchangeability and encourage role change for skilled employees and enhanced social capital.

Poor intellectual capital management practices and inadequate leadership strategies erode social capital, which can result in considerable frustration and stress.[26] As a core condition for the successful contribution of intellectual capital to creativity and innovation, there is a need for organisations to restrict social capital erosion. Social capital interactions facilitate the creation and transfer of tacit knowledge, which along, with intellectual capital, complexly link to social capital and thereby influence intellectual capital creation. Social capital erosion therefore results in lost opportunities to capitalise on organic creativity and innovation.[27] However, adaptable and flexible social structures that successfully foster and harness social capital assist organisations to become competitive, creative and innovative. Flexible social structures result from networked associations, so organisations must therefore foster environments that concurrently encourage human and social capital growth.[28]

Part Five: Structural Capital

31. Organisational Characteristics

Organisational characteristics generally relate to an internal context in which organisational structures or management that influence these characteristics have a critical effect on organically generated creativity and innovation. This section considers such aspects relevant to creativity and innovation including culture, emergent properties, knowledge management and organisational improvement.

32. Resources

Complex global environments place intense demands on finite resources, which require informed economic decisions for survival.[1] Such complex situations of high demand and scarce resources put pressure on organisations to adapt and improve[2] because value creation within organisations leads to efficiencies and well-utilised resources.

Exchanges of agential tacit knowledge are necessary for knowledge development and combination.[3] However, agential ethnicity and organisational cultures influence control, recognition and retrieval of tacit knowledge, which creates reward structures and facilitates individuals' retention and competition.[4] Thus, agential collaboration rather than competition will benefit organisations.[5] Further, teams that function well have synergistic influences on organisational effectiveness which reduce tension and make up for shortfalls of individual team members. Consequently, the promotion of teamwork and cross-functional teams capitalises on inherent synergies in diverse organisational cultures.

An explicit transparent process is required to develop innovative ideas within organisations. When departments operate as silos, innovation lacks encouragement and importance, which hinders the distribution of ideas. Organisations also need to ensure the responsible and adequate employment of scarce resources because the scarcity of departmental resources can cause issues with skill management and utilisation. Further, the absence of formal team interactions within organisations usually results from budget constraints, a lack of financial and human resources, and from which a lack of teamwork and budget overruns result in silos rather than teams.

Individuals who do not meet role requirements or who struggle with role demands require a significant time investment because agents need to be performance managed, which puts undue pressure on managers, the team and damages morale. Thus, previous work relationships allow for skillsets to be understood, which ensures the recruitment of the right people. Conversely, good interviewers also require the skill and ability to recognise aptitudes of potential employees to innovate, which can be valuable to the organisation. As previously discussed, high staff turnover also creates issues of knowledge retention and retraining, which constrains the level of service provided. Additionally, the quality and type of knowledge retention within organisations is critical. Therefore, the choices of persons to performance manage or make redundant in times of crisis remains a challenging responsibility of management.

The availability of internal resources within organisations affects intrinsic agential motivation to engage in creative and innovative behaviours. However, some individuals are naturally productive as they professionally challenge and approach traditional solutions creatively and innovatively, with no expectation of financial reward. Providing challenges for agents through annual performance plans can foster an environment of creativity and result in functional participation because agents occasionally need encouragement to get started. Besides, agents can foster an innovative environment through their self-development initiatives because they can utilise the resources provided to them to help people bond and boost general morale within the organisation.

Occasionally, organisations choose to engage contractors and consultants because they do not internally possess the required skills. Thus, the regular engagement of such specialised contractors who provide an all-round service remains the most efficient. Repeat engagement also allows for effective organisational knowledge retention. Consequently, intellectual property (IP) ownership for consultants' work is an issue because the IP may belong to the consultant. IP ownership presents a critical knowledge retention risk for organisations with external knowledge stores. Competitors can easily purchase this knowledge, which makes it widely available and non-exclusive to organisations. The increased use of consultants can also be exorbitantly expensive for organisations, which makes staff retention a more cost-effective strategy.

Agents with a wide variety of skills allow for continuity during periods of employee leave or sickness. Work variety increases agential engagement, interest and responsibility to promote retention and effective knowledge distribution. Additionally, teamwork, time-share, and skills matching ensure teams function more effectively. Agential experience supports associations with new challenges thus, a capitalised prior professional relationship can help to preserve intellectual capital. Although teamwork can be challenging and uncomfortable, an established agential base fosters relationships and builds a stronger team. Agents should also be upskilled and provided with opportunities that challenge them to lessen the risk of demotivation which forces them to look externally for career opportunities.

Organisations need data to convert ideas into innovation. However, in many organisations, no specific practice exists that agents can adapt to become innovative because creativity emerges from arbitrary processes. Although micromanagement does not support agential task completion, some task guidance empowers agents to seek further clarification or direction as needed. A good record of accomplishment with management allows agents' work ethic to be recognised, which permits acceptance in the event of a crisis. In most organisations, senior management generally remain open to financially justified ideas. However, during a resources downturn, analysis to justify creative and innovative ideas can be difficult because feasibility studies also require an investment of funds and other scarce resources.

33. Utilising

Management has a responsibility to allocate scarce resources such as staffing and funding to ensure efficient application.[1] Scarcity in financial resources results from economic climates, thus organisational agents should only undertake viable projects. Organisations also effectively operate and allocate staffing as inventory[2] and employ consultants or short-term contractors as required to close skills gaps. However, an on-board impost on such transient agents exists and indicates that a collective effort towards staff retention may be economical. An organisational need to facilitate and provide resources for activities that increase external networks in which tangible organisational benefits emerge exists.

Leaders have a responsibility to assist with workload management and enable space[3] to address situations in which agents externalise and blame a heavy workload for missed opportunities for creative endeavours.[4] Due to excessive workload, agents' may also lack needed resources to accommodate stakeholders with more timely information. Thus, the redistribution and reallocation of workload across available resources enable reflection space for process improvement, which becomes easier among multi-skilled and experienced agents. Increased workload often creates situations where agents seek suboptimal solutions to problems rather than take the time to reflect and understand underlying causes,[5] which results in a shallow process familiarity and knowledge outcomes.[6]

Instability and a constant flux state result in the inability to accrue new knowledge and override improvements, which makes it costly to capitalise on innovation with a first-mover advantage.[7] Some organisational areas can also dynamically change to meet current information demand, with the expectation that this supports specific individual needs for efficient performance. A response in this manner enhances the job security of agents, although it does so with adverse implications for workloads and a deeper comprehension of process effectiveness in service areas. Thus, organisations need to facilitate workload management to ensure that agents have time to reflect on their work and processes. Further, reflection assists organisations to be open to innovative ideas.

34. Culture

Culture is conceptual, though the intense power that emerges from social interactions operates outside general awareness, the cultural concept serves to explain and standardise such energy.[1] Additionally, personal and organisational belief structures drive replication and incorporation and also influence motivational factors that encourage knowledge transfer within organisations.[2] Research on cultural differences between nations identifies five independent dimensions:

1. 'power distance,
2. individualism or collectivism,
3. masculinity or femininity,
4. long-term or short-term orientation and
5. uncertainty avoidance'.[3]

Belief structures influence knowledge creation and transfer within organisations, which take the form of standards, rules and recognised practices known as organisational culture.[4] However, a significant historical and cultural understanding of the local economic, political, social and cultural conditions in specific countries is needed to understand prevalent management processes, philosophies and problems in these countries.[5]

Organisational climate is linked to agential behaviour and reflects a cultural situation at a specific point in time that emerges as a complex view of entrenched distinct circumstances, making culture permanent.[6] Climate occurs as common observation and the sense that agents create and attach to organisational policies and modes of operation, which includes agential behaviour that management encourages and rewards.[7] Climate can support creativity and innovation because it enhances agential inventiveness, which results from an increased focus on the innovation environment.[8] Climate also emerges from agential interaction and communication,[9] with agents increasingly affected when creativity occurs organically.[10]

Culture can foster or hinder knowledge activity and control

knowledge-related behaviours,[11] which determines the quantity and quality of knowledge shared.[12] However, organisational culture remains sensitive to **change through influence**[13] **to make trust,**[14] **openness and uncertainty acceptance**[15] important aspects that transform knowledge creation and transfer. Consequently, a focus on internal culture to effectively harness it for competitive advantage is crucial.[16]

Culture shapes assumptions of knowledge, which facilitate relationships, interactions, and establish procedures that influence knowledge creation and distribution.[17] Organisational attitudes and culture also affect agential risk tendency and eagerness to partake in knowledge creation, with culture influencing role clarity where situations are ambiguous.[18]

35. Receptive and Supportive

There is a need for organisational leaders to be effective communicators and create conditions for idea generation to facilitate creativity and innovation. However, management may not always be receptive to new ideas, although sessions to canvass innovative ideas on adaptive challenges are beneficial. Similarly, consultancy firms use interdisciplinary groups to garner diverse views, which assist with creativity and innovation. However, the employment of interdisciplinary groups to garner views remains uncharacteristic and unlikely to work for organisations within the resource sector as they are generally blue-collar site roles geared narrowly towards resource production. Thus, management needs to provide support and resources to complete tasks and engage the external mind when the organisation does not have the required in-house skills.

Networks help organisations recruit prospective employees through industry connections rather than adverts. Thus, regular association with prior employees also allows organisations and agents to keep abreast of external opportunities as well as the availability of previously employed agents with in-demand skills. Agentially, those with management credibility, recognition of continuous contribution and performance also have some leeway to make occasional errors in the organic innovation space. Though, sound business cases that support ideas can aid in promoting such ideas to management for consideration. However, in a resources sector downturn, financial resources need to be prioritised and although difficult, ideas need support, which results in tension because a scarcity of funds exists to support ideas that can benefit organisations.

Social networks also remain a different ideology in non-Western organisations which some management do not consider add value to the business. Thus, different ideologies combined with a lack of dedicated departments to investigate, process, publicise and implement innovation can be a further reason for new ideas not being followed through to implementation. Similarly, the internal cultural aspects of organisations serve to affect extrinsic agential motivations to engage in creative and innovative behaviour, in which recognition and reward encourage creativity and innovation but remain as an expected part of most jobs rather than being dependent on particular skill or effort.

The absence of recognition, encouragement for creativity and innovation, or the provision of visible incentives and bonuses through formalised reward structures do not reward or reflect agential performance. Further, some organisations take agential contributions for granted and provide no guidance or encouragement for creativity and innovation. Such management behaviour can lead to learned helplessness and cause agents to wonder why they continue to be creative. Conversely, motivated agents perform at a higher level and tend to be innovative regardless of external encouragement. However, acknowledgement encourages agents to be increasingly creative and innovative, especially when the agential contribution is immediately acknowledged, which helps to motivate and incentivise them.

Centres of excellence, such as business improvement departments, are also symbolic within organisations due to their visibility across departments and hierarchy levels of the organisation, as well as their ability to dismantle silo cultures. Centres such as these can foster relationships, encourage and reward creativity and innovation. Thus, organisations can lose a potentially rich source of ideas without the existence of such centres of excellence. Role and responsibility uncertainty, as well as a silo culture, can result from a lack of organisational structure and communication.

The resources sector faces a further critical issue: the lack of innovation during the feasibility and implementation stage, which commits the organisation to inflexible modes of operation during the short term. Although diverse employee groups can encourage and foster innovation, the resources industry does not make use of such diversity, which additionally reduces the scope for out-of-the-box innovation.

Trust is another core condition for knowledge distribution because taking credit and assuming ownership for someone's idea creates distrust and reluctance to share. Due to constrained multinational organisational structures, promotion as a reward and recognition practice for the performance of long-tenured agents can be limited. Conversely, failure to recognise good ideas also manifests into a no consequence for bad ideas or decisions culture.

A core issue for multinational organisations is the amount of rework and reconstruction required to comply with local regulations. Rework generally results from a lack of proper feasibility studies performed on Greenfield operations in which operational management do not understand the local environments, resulting in adverse consequences due to the exploits of other organisations. The risk of repeat errors also exists, which results in corrective work that exacerbates when agents remain unanswerable.

Additionally, the internal culture of organisations regarding recognition and reward affects intrinsic agential motivations to engage in creative and innovative behaviours. Thus, when agents take risks, sacrifice personal time and resources for betterment through self-development, support from management is vital to ensure successful completion of these development initiatives, which are an essential source of new organic knowledge. Occasionally, self-development initiatives can create bitterness and threat amongst agents when someone else tries to develop their skills because they may become subordinated. However, people with the right skills and will to self-develop through continuous improvement activities are innately creative and innovative and can capitalise on first-mover advantage within the sector. Continuous improvement also occurs as a very repetitive process, which enhances activities efficiently.

The internal organisational culture builds trust and affects intrinsic agential motivations to engage in creative and innovative behaviours. Thus, facilitating processes for agents to complete tasks as they see fit allows them to develop efficient methods of issue resolution and task completion. In this manner, agentic empowerment in various forms provides task ownership and motivates agents to engage functionally with organisational values that support individual responsibilities. Consequently, the delegation and distribution of tasks through empowerment also allow individuals to have ownership, responsibility and the freedom to manage processes enabling creativity and innovation to emerge.

36. Risk

Self-development occurs when agents recognise the need for further improvement, have the control to select the type of development and willingly undertake the required knowledge to drive initiatives.[1] However, few managers support agents who take professional or personal risks and further develop their non-mandatory skillset.

Thus, support from management is essential for self-development to be successful because management risks the loss of accumulated tacit knowledge. During boom times, most organisations sponsor self-development initiatives and generally reimburse a portion of course fees for formal education; however, organisations usually provide this with a catch that locks agents into the organisation for several years following course completion. To encourage self-development, organisations will benefit from the reinstatement of unconstrained agential support.

37. Awareness

A fundamental dilemma to understand and recognise patterns of self-organisation exists. This dilemma becomes epistemological because it relates to a knowing capability[1] and the ability to notice unexpected patterns of behaviour.[2]

In addition to personnel and industry awareness, management needs to ensure that they do not sabotage or set agents up for failure. Conversely, agents should proactively recognise areas of improvement and take the initiative to be creative and innovative. Although cultural diversity creates tension between non-Western and Western management ideologies, there is an appreciation of the need for confidentiality. However, such awareness becomes challenging because organisational and personal issues can collectively affect or be affected by the organisation.

Fundamental to their effectiveness, organisations need to ensure that they maintain statutory and regulatory occupational health and safety standards and provide a safe work environment.[3] Consequently, organisations need to ensure they treat agents with care and respect. Inappropriate treatment of people, public reprimands, and then truthful expectations from staff displays a lack of agential respect and awareness, which results in voice suppression and withheld information.

38. Knowledge Management

Knowledge management is the productive, efficient use of organisational knowledge sources and resources, with the current global environment dictating that knowledge worker efficiency is increasingly more valuable than production assets.[1] Thus, to sustain long-term competitive advantage, organisational ability to manage knowledge is a core competence.[2] Consequently, increases in knowledge assets will likely lead to increased organisational learning[3] as well as creativity and innovation. Although, organisational knowledge needs to be managed, harnessed, widely distributed and shared to resolve uncertain and significant issues in a timely fashion and promote knowledge creation.[4]

Innovative understanding becomes indispensable because organisational learning is dynamically charged and continually evolving. [5] Thus, the productive use of knowledge to achieve organisational goals is critical and requires effective knowledge management,[6] which fosters agential knowledge internalisation.[7] Organisationally, this becomes an essential risk management strategy which allows vital knowledge to be shared to minimise the risk of knowledge erosion,[8] and in the process builds redundancy within the organisation.[9]

Knowledge management represents a progression through recurring and evolving dynamic complex interactions,[10] a potent social process that considers human and social factors.[11] A process that emerges and interconnects to organisational social and knowledge activities[12] with four vital components,[13] knowledge management takes the form of **creation, recognition, transfer and internalisation**.[14] Knowledge creation incorporates experience that socially constructs through interactions and[15] consolidates inorganically acquired and organically generated knowledge. Knowledge is **codified, shared, internalised and manifested** through agential interactions that achieve organisational goals.[16]

In global organisations, knowledge management faces six main challenges:

1. context,
2. tacitness,
3. technology,
4. staff and diversity strategies,
5. organisational structure and
6. complexities of globalisation.[17]

Knowledge management results in creativity that operates on the border of disorder due to the inherent uncertain and dynamic nature of knowledge.[18] Creativity results from systems that operate between **stability and instability or between predictability and unpredictability**[19] to exhibit tension and attractor dynamics between these two extremes.

Organisations with a focus on knowledge management often treat tacit knowledge as valuable and foster interactions and relationships to create, improve and share this knowledge. Such organisations frequently generate and employ social capital from agential interactions to replicate and shape organisational intellectual capital.[20] Thus, a new culture, practices and reward systems execute to enhance such social relationships.[21] Tacit knowledge is relevant because it is:

- context-specific,
- novel,
- challenging to duplicate,
- readily usable and
- grounded in complex organisational dynamics.

Similarly, knowledge acquisition requires organisations to relive comparable experiences, which entail considerable time and resource investment.[22]

The internal organisational environment influences creativity and innovation in which directions from management serve to affect intrinsic agential motivations to engage in creative and innovative behaviours. For example, centres of excellence create high symbolism due to their visibility across all hierarchy levels, their ability to communicate improvements throughout the organisation and dismantle silos. Such centres generally collate, review, analyse and reward new ideas to enhance organisational performance. An absence of centres of excellence results in missed innovation potential as an organisation loses the opportunity to acknowledge and act on creativity. A silo culture can also result because organisations do not dissipate solutions to common problems across the organisation.

The absence of a common language within organisations excludes people from conversations, impacts effective communication, and influences and restricts task completion. Organisations also need frequent and prominent business communication to avoid agents resorting to online news. Thus, sanctioned communication in a majority language–English in most cases–is preferred because reliance on unreliable online translation tools can result in distorted meaning. A further loss in translation can result from missed language nuances as well as visible facial and hand expressions generated during verbal communications. Additionally, essentialism between diverse cultures can result in tension with the potential for synergistic effect when organisations bring diverse cultures together through different paradigms.

Divisions of foreign-owned conglomerates can have distinct cultural groups with non-Western and Western styles of communication, leadership, language and identities. Such cultural groups can create organisational identity issues with an operating philosophy that naturally flows once the organisation establishes a unique identity through the extraction and combination of cultural elements. Cultural and communication issues create challenges within organisational hierarchies that comprise of excessive director levels, sometimes with unwarranted positions. In divisions of foreign-owned conglomerates, directors from different cultural backgrounds bring different management styles and seldom consider the long-term consequences of their actions.

A lack of transparency and communication from upper management affects decisions made at different levels within organisations, sometimes with an influence that may lack effective leadership and organisational objectives that the organisation can validate. Multinational organisations can experience problems in establishing operations in unknown environments, which correlate with choosing expatriate construction organisations that do not have any local construction experience, making management of the construction phase difficult.

At lower levels, unawareness of or feedback on what drives organisational strategic plans creates uncertainty because higher levels may ignore information and ideas that lower levels supply. Conversely, a lack of feedback can occasionally stimulate and encourage the generation of new ideas. However, in the longer term, a lack of feedback tends to demotivate and discourage.

In most cases, continuous process improvement supports organisational operations in their current life cycle stages. However, although evolved from inception, organisations may still utilise outdated practices. Additionally, controlling budgets and costs become harder when people do not understand the financial value of initiatives. Thus, studies to justify investment are essential because agents sometimes thoughtlessly expend organisational resources.

39. Organisational Knowledge

Organisations can observe the consequences of agential knowledge in associations and thoroughness of information, distribution, development, internalisation, and interpretation.[1] Awareness helps to recognise and correct mistakes[2] where the lack of either inhibits improvement. Thus, the need for reform intensifies in uncertain and dynamic environments, which increases the complexity of effective and efficient organisational knowledge.[3] Two significant variables that organisations can reconstruct internally address such challenges to make effective decisions. These variables are the:

- timeliness of information and
- receptivity to corrective feedback.[4]

Corrective actions can occur through single-loop or double-loop feedback and knowledge systems.

Single-loop and double-loop learning perform significant functions in organisational improvement. In isolation, single-loop learning occurs when agents undertake corrective action to predetermined variables that define actions. Whereas, double-loop learning occurs when agents reflexively question predetermined variables and take previously undefined corrective action.[5] Single-loop learning results from organisational support and encouragement of improvement so long as primary goals, behaviours and activities remain unchallenged.[6] Conversely, double-loop learning occurs when organisations challenge primary goals, actions and pursuits[7] to become increasingly adaptive. Thus, single-loop is evolutionary in which organisations respond slowly to changes, whereas double-loop learning is revolutionary, transforms organisations,[8] and is agentially driven.

Characteristically, organisations in the natural resources sector attempt to value-add to a homogenous commodity, which makes product differentiation difficult. Homogeneity makes the sector extremely price-sensitive, with cost-effectiveness a higher preference.[9] Thus, when organisations do not identify and address knowledge and improvement gaps, knowledge is weakened, which results in suboptimal decisions[10] and the loss of innovation. Consequently, organisations effectively integrate knowledge when they can address knowledge and improvement gaps,[11] which push organisations into a state of equilibrium[12] to foster and create innovative opportunities.

Three methods achieve creativity: **chance, conformity and intervention**,[13] in which agents link associated components.

Consequently, increased agential associations with current problems create mediating bridges through element aggregation which can result in creative solutions.[14] Consequently, associative or tacit knowledge sources through experience,[15] and engages agents to associate with different events.[16] During this process, agential awareness emerges through associations that bridge current situations with prior experience, which consequently enhances knowledge through preserved memory.[17]

Knowledge management is critical to nurture innovative behaviour because agents dissipate vital intelligence and energy to understand unfamiliar environmental concepts.[18] Thus, crucial task-specific knowledge develops through experience[19] when agents exercise skills that involve significant tacit knowledge, which can limit organisational capacity to internalise applied skills.[20]

Tacit awareness empowers agents to create previously unconsidered links and associations to challenges that result in creativity. Consequently, the core of expertise lies in the knowledge that agents carry regarding these links and associations.[21] Tacit knowledge codification results from agential motivation or coercion and recognition and reward systems to increase production ability and allow assimilation of know-how, which makes knowledge diversity important.[22] However, creative capacity emerges from exposure to experience and knowledge management, access to tacit awareness as well as application and effort.[23]

Knowledge generates through organisational adaptiveness and the application of emergent learning to create new products and services. Although, organisations can instead maintain homeostasis and apply adaptive expertise to manage and survive with their current products and services.[24] Generative knowledge occurs as a paradigm shift, in which organisations consider current products, systems, processes and activities differently and improve them to meet unacknowledged customer needs. Conversely, adaptive knowledge results when organisations fail to detect challenge causes and force traits rather than eliminate reasons.[25] From an agential perspective, organisational agents can be adaptive if their actions attribute value that increases over time with behaviour. Thus, organisations have to create and refine their employee value propositions to attract and retain skilled people as well as invest in agential development.[26]

A critical literature review of organisational learning highlights that organisational knowledge does not compile individual knowledge processes, but instead steadily engages agentially and with the external mind.[27] Additionally, due to downturns, reorganisations and cutbacks, returns on training investments can be unclear, which result in discontinued organisational training programs.[28] Thus, training frameworks need to include a strategic focus on creativity and innovation to sustain competitive advantage.[29]

40. Tacit Knowledge

Tacit knowledge refers to the uncodified skills and experience of collective organisational processes that employees possess. Tacit knowledge informally emerges and contains intangible forms such as **proficiency, judgement, awareness, experience and tricks of the trade**. Inherent challenges to codify and communicate tacit knowledge cause organisations to struggle to motivate and encourage employees to share their knowledge.[1] Thus, with explicit awareness already known and readily available to others, organisations can only achieve competitive advantage through tacit knowledge.[2]

Tacit awareness requires direct experience and interaction due to a very steep 'distance decay' curve,[3] that is, as the distance from the context increases, experience and interaction declines thereby making organisational knowledge context-specific, implicit or tacit dependent. Thus, tacit knowledge is difficult to articulate, codify and imitate,[4] devaluing and losing its essence when separated from core context.[5] Personal commitment and identification with the organisational mission are also fundamental to access tacit knowledge and make it available for further development.[6] With a high turnover rate, the resources sector experiences tacit knowledge erosion and consequently, organisational knowledge retention through staff retention and recognition of worth and value-add is essential.

An alternative view to turnover problems considers how agential tenure ultimately affects performance because agents tend to become stagnant, comfortable and complacent in organisational processes and therefore resist change efforts and opportunities to improve.[7] Long-term tenure does not hinder young organisations because agents seek other opportunities either voluntarily or through redundancies. However, organisations should attempt to retain agents if they have the required skill set and fit for the organisation.

Alternatively, by developing effective individual performance rank systems,[8] organisations should identify and address the underlying causes of underperformance instead of termination. Thus, staff retention should be a priority to keep current organisational knowledge because an increase in forced or voluntary turnover involves a cost to on-board and train,[9] which produces a training liability for organisations.

A process, methods, systems and tools approach to codifying, managing and capitalising knowledge is not suited to tacit knowledge.[10] Thus, some generic strategies to codify tacit context-specific knowledge are team attendance and participation in training or conferences for agents to subsequently share the understanding gained from their knowledge.

The need to be creative results from the desire to improve because each agential interaction transpires to build relationships and provide opportunities for improvement through further knowledge.[11] Organisations should therefore encourage agential interactions through brainstorming because these generate creativity.[12] However, brainstorming can be restrictive because creativity emerges as a by-product of playful activity unrestricted by hierarchies or limitations set by management with brainstorming generally occurring with constraints. Attitudes and views within brainstorming sessions also tend to gravitate towards prevailing group attitudes.[13] As such, support converges towards the most dominant view,[14] which can identify nonoptimal solutions to achieve majority consensus,[15] and become organisational challenges.

Psychological and socio-psychological issues in organisations[16] include **team stereotypes, makeup, culture, responsibility and essentialism**. Culture enables or hinders leadership and agential interactions with differences and communication styles that play significant roles in the effective management of multicultural environments.[17] Misinterpretations and ineffective communication which results from cultural differences collectively inhibit and restrict problem understanding and resolution.[18]

Culture forms through the assumptions, beliefs and values agentially shared that sometimes identify as strong or thick and are essential parts of organisational functions and mechanisms.[19] The existence of standards and customs, which employees at all levels share[20], allow organisations to differentiate from other cultures[21] and ensure non-deviation from the norm. Even in their adopted environments, multinational organisations sometimes operate instinctively through home cultural aspects in which preferred agents receive higher management positions through the imported culture and organisational setup.

Accountability within organisations is essential because it depicts an image of transparency and trust.[22] In this respect, organisations need to introduce some agential decision responsibility to avoid the repetition of mistakes. Conversely, to continually assist and improve operations, organisations also need to increase management accountability and learn lessons from their adverse decisions. Thus, the opportunity to take responsibility and ownership of tasks motivates and fosters an environment of trust, which reduces the need to continually monitor processes.[23] Trust creates circumstances to generate and nurture creativity and innovation. The absence of ownership can, however, contribute to an environment of uncertainty.

41. Emergent Properties

Properties that develop when organisations enable dynamic processes, explain complexity in the system.[1] Thus, emergent properties occur as new properties that crystallise or emerge from interplays between organisational components, but which do not exist independently.[2] Interactions of different complexity can be at the agential level or the agential and organisational levels. Consequently, emergent properties have a synergistic influence on systems.

Self-organisation in dynamic processes can produce autocatalysis or emergent properties. These properties enable growth[3] or disequilibrium energy dispersion,[4] which creates adaptive change.[5] Emergent properties arise from instability,[6] in which sudden unpredictable changes exhibit at the granular or agential level,[7] interactions and energic pressures.[8]

Emergent properties yield mechanisms that explain manifested change events.[9] Such mechanisms remain fundamental to information flows and facilitate recognisable patterns across diverse situations, which provides answers when organisations cannot identify specific causes and effects.

Creativity, innovation and adaptability within organisations[10] emerge through mechanisms such as attractors, storytelling, bonding, attention patterning, elaboration, and conflicting constraint.[11] Thus, in the process, agents resonate,[12] associate, and bond to change their views to a typical group inter-resonance structure.[13] Consequently, resonance results from behaviours of interdependent agents acting dependently[14] to realise a collective need.[15]

Interactions display intense, dynamic properties[16] to create a higher-order system which when synchronised agentially[17] exhibits emergent properties.[18] Synchronisation results from a change in agential thoughts, feelings and their inclination to act, which encourages a mutual agential reality.[19]

Although vastly different, interactions, resonance and synchronisation mirror similar processes in which resonance forces the behavioural change of interdependent agents and then reverts to its original state once the interaction ceases. Whereas synchronisation dynamically occurs as a complex process in which independent agents continue to change and match their behaviours.[20]

42. Emergence

Regarded as the anchor point phenomenon of complexity theory,[1] emergence results from agential interdependency[2] that occurs at lower organisational levels when agents interact and resonate through networks and exchange information, take action and adapt to feedback. Agential interdependency encourages knowledge and pressures agents to act on knowledge flows within organisations.[3] Consequently, agents who learn faster than others in the team become a focus for the 'basin of attraction' that emerges,[4] and in the process, they accumulate expert power and become emergent leaders.[5]

Taking an initial step towards process reform does not matter because improvement through trial and error can generate creative ideas. Thus, adaptation occurs through experimentation,[6] which effectively channels this energy to become vital to the generation of creativity, innovation and adaptive knowledge.[7] Consequently, mechanisms occur as universally available emergent patterns of behaviour, which enable a specific dynamic mix of variables and causal chains that explain events with attractors which manifest as one of six mechanisms to foster adaptability and creativity.[8] Additionally, creativity and innovation also occur as mechanisms through the emergence of new ideas and the willingness of agents to act.

Part Six: Social Capital

Elements of adaptive leadership exist alongside cybernetic leadership practices in many organisations. However, factors that hinder or foster creativity and innovation suggest that turnover and the use of transient employees requires careful management because they introduce an element of instability in the social capital base of organisations.

As an asset, social capital anchors in agential relationships,[1] with an inherent characteristic of awareness that evolves through agential interactivity or through agential groups who do not follow predetermined rules.[2] Thus, investments in social capital require the development of processes which encourage agential interactions, build relationships, teamwork and cooperation.[3] Social capital positively affects the ability of organisations to stimulate agential commitment, increase agential flexibility, manage collective action and develop high levels of intellectual capital.[4] Additionally, agents in such relationships maintain mutual social capital and so no single party has exclusivity over this asset.[5]

In young organisations with high turnover rates and short tenure agents, it is a challenge to build relationships that positively add value. Consequently, a high organisational turnover rate makes it beneficial to facilitate synergies that increase the chances of developing long-term relationships and to organically increase social capital. Therefore, tension exists between the need to increase social capital through interaction and tenure management in organisations.

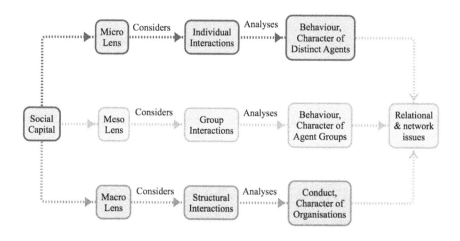

Figure 6.1: Analytical Lenses

Social capital 'micro' interactions occur as individual interactions in nature, 'meso' are group interactions and 'macro' interactions encompass social structures and societies.[6] Organisational social capital interactions reflect a meso and a micro lens, where a meso lens focus is on relational and network issues and a micro lens focuses on psychological and socio-psychological issues.[7]

The use of a micro and a meso lens is appropriate to consider interactions focusing on the behaviour and character of distinct agents and agents within group environments, whereas the macro lens focuses on conduct and character of organisations. The meso lens focuses on a combination of both the micro and macro lenses.[8]

43. Meso

A meso perspective analyses relational and network issues,[1] which encompass an awareness of how organisations relate to and appreciate agential participation and acknowledge, recognise, reward and promote agents for their efforts. The nurture of relationships also involves the setup of networks that engage with the external mind. Organisations can allow internal agents to cross-fertilise or exchange ideas and opinions with agents from other organisations, which can develop novel solutions to current challenges. For example, attendance at conferences to learn about environmental innovation and target previously utilised reputable consultants can also assist engagement with the external mind.

Management can facilitate conditions that support network formation and provide a required structure in the form of decision ability and autonomy that allow such systems to face organisational challenges.[2] Goal-directedness and serendipitous processes occur as two network solutions that explain node restructure and addition[3] as well as preferred links in which new nodes connect with other favoured nodes.[4] Nodes can also take the form of new projects, challenges, members or methods.[5]

Network interactions enable organisations to acquire awareness and effectively internalise it, with agential talent recommendations allowing organisations to tap into the hidden talent market. Compatibility encourages organisational and social relationships to thrive through candid conversations[6] with personal relationships that help to develop and establish healthy professional foundations in organisations. A previous employment history or relationship also assists connections to build and maintain current rapport, which allows agents to cooperate and work together effectively. Consequently, the degree of social capital within organisations can determine organisational success, with social capital levels being proportional to organisational success.[7]

Social capital develops based on reciprocity within relationships and can dissolve once the relationship ceases.[8] The 'weak tie theory' suggests that agential connections, with occasional interactions outside current networks, usually have better access to rare intelligence and resources, which can provide instant insights into external work practices or job opportunities.[9] 'Weak tie theory' is organisationally correlated because external mind connections empower agents to keep abreast of industry innovation. External network connections can also help identify applicants suitable for vacant organisational roles without wasting recruitment budgets.

Organic creativity and innovation require robust inorganic relationships to thrive. However, over-dependence on inorganic relationships can be constraining because trust generates tension when the external mind retains innovation-related knowledge and skills. Consequently, organisations critically need to cultivate creativity and innovation but also internalise such knowledge.

44. Macro

A macro or a micro perspective can support complex systems because individual agential choice that is at the micro level determines their macro behaviours.[1] Thus, macro structures can explain agential interactions, which provide an awareness of the interaction context. The presence of choice, as well as needs inconsistency, ensures that agential interactions remain unpredictable.[2] As with social capital, the macro lens deals with the conduct and character of organisations.[3] Macro behaviours remain rational so long as they contribute towards the anticipated value for individuals at a micro-level.[4]

Greenfield operations in relatively unknown geographical and economic environments create numerous organisational challenges such as an awareness of the local regulatory and statutory environment, awareness of the importance of the local indigenous customs, as well as how to deal with budgetary constraints that result from labour and material shortages. Over time, when such systems become tense or unstable, there is often a dramatic and sudden release of energy, which creates unexpected systemic order or emergent outcomes that can be creative.[5]

Organisations can handle conflict and maintain a competitive advantage when they harness and channel energy released from innovative activities and are flexible with dynamic change. A continuous focus on control and compliance, therefore, drains leadership energy, whereas emergent leadership recognises that organisations cannot avoid internal conflict. Emergent leadership energises and encourages free information flows[6] to make organisations adaptable to change.

Adaptive systems shift and move around landscapes with diverse possibilities or 'attractor pits', which represent organisational strategies that can lead to unexpected system changes.[7] Adaptability fosters better ways or a continuous improvement environment that usually results in more reliable data as well as cost efficiencies. Efficient knowledge distribution and transfer are critical in organisations, as is the ability to learn on the job through identification and improvement of current processes, which influences productivity and optimises operational efficiency. However, the resources sector inherently engages in process enhancement, although it uses technologically advanced equipment with innovation comparable to other manufacturing industries. Consequently, the resources sector cannot be a classed as a high-tech industry.[8] Selectivity about resourcing organisational projects is critical to be innovative and foster an environment of continuous improvement. Resources include time and staff support to identify, develop and pursue opportunities or additional financial resources to tap into the external mind. A lack of financial resources or labour and skills to perform day-to-day activities generates tension because such resources are critical for agents to foster creativity and innovation.

45. Diversity

Diversity creates the disparity that many believe ignites innovative thought.[1] Heterogeneity and synergy[2] generate innovative solutions in which agents address challenges that result in in-group creativity.[3] Due to increased globalisation and uncertainty, particularly after the GFC, recruitment from diverse cultures, experiences and ethnic backgrounds became essential. In an organisational context, to facilitate and foster innovation and knowledge, different agential values, assumptions, beliefs and work habits are invaluable.[4] Simultaneously, effective management of such diversity is necessary to ensure that diversity does not hinder the generation of creativity and innovation.[5]

Organisational diversity presents in many different ways including race, gender, sexual orientation, cultural differences, education, analytical skillsets and language. Agential interactions can encourage or discourage diverse preferences, views, attitudes, duties, awareness and habits.[6] Predominantly, the diversity of cultural differences and language is considered because these factors directly affect creative tension, which organisations need to manage in knowledge codification, transfer and interactions. A lack of research currently exists on interpersonal communication in organisations with a diverse workforce,[7] which highlights a gap in how organisations can understand the impact of interpersonal communication on organisational sustainability.

A complex system view stresses and values interdependency and diversity within organisations.[8] In multinational organisations, cultural diversity influences locational inclusivity between cultures and across geographical locations.[9] Thus, to harness the potential and consequent sustainability of creativity and innovation from diverse cultures is a challenge faced by multinational organisations because of the difficulties that result from essentialism and thin communication. Consequently, tension exists in the selection of effective methods to manage diversity that fosters rather than hinders creativity. As such, heterogeneity can be a double-edged sword[10] because diversity functions in distinct ways in varied situations, which makes it crucial to understand the analytical context.[11]

Multinational organisations also possess differences in culture, leadership, management styles and general operating modes, which create difficulties for locally recruited staff that have to adapt to different leadership styles and management behaviours. Challenges of the local context also exist for multinationals, including differences in physical environments, additional stringent regulations, policies and work ethics. There is a risk of potential essentialism in cultural analysis because global organisations cannot adequately express the cultures of typical individuals.[12]

Intercultural communication becomes increasingly important to gain a competitive advantage in a globalised business environment,[13] which requires organisations to have the capability to interact with agents from diverse backgrounds and cultures.[14] Personality and trait theory generally accepts the five-factor model of personalities, which they commonly refer to as the 'Big Five'.[15] McAdams and Pals explain:

"The Big Five broadly organises individual differences in social and

emotional life into five factor-analytically-derived categories, most commonly labelled extraversion (vs. introversion), neuroticism (negative affectivity), conscientiousness, agreeableness, and openness to experience.[16]"

Differences in personalities, language, communication styles and other inherent issues that result from thin communication affect the organisational ability to function effectively in global markets. In global organisations, agents educated through different processes, cultures and traditions interact,[17] which can result in cross-cultural misinterpretation. However, although personality psychology has seen remarkable progress, it has not clearly explained or provided a structure to help in fully comprehending individual persons.[18]

The potential lack of a common language and inherent communication differences have adverse implications for expatriates in foreign countries who may not be able to resonate and satisfactorily express themselves.[19] Thus, a reduced ability to socialise, share stories or codify knowledge are some negative consequences of thin communication and essentialism[20] that adversely affect multinational organisations trying to nurture environments favourable to creativity and innovation .

Part Seven: Relational Capital

46. Characteristics

Much of the academic literature focuses on agential characteristics, their importance for creativity and innovation, and how these characteristics assist in interaction. Conversely, relational aspects are essential to organisational knowledge flows. I broadly group and discuss these below under the headings of managed socialisation, agential interactions and communications.

Relational characteristics occur as resources linked to external relationships such as suppliers, partners, consultants, contractors and customers.[1] Relational capital relates to a bond between internal or external customers that manifests through selfless agential acts to benefit, promote and defend organisations.[2] Intellectual capital results from agential competence and commitment, thus containing organisational knowledge leakage.[3] Intricate contacts shape agential relationships and the external mind[4] with emergent leaders fostering relationships to increase capability, interactions and connections. Thus, organic support arises from positive interactions or as agential rapport, which makes agents appear as friendly and trustworthy through demonstrated loyalty.[5]

47. Managed Socialisation

To foster informal leadership, engage, motivate, and sustain action to develop awareness and talents is challenging. However, sharing nurtures through a demonstrated capacity to engage beyond immediate agential roles,[1] with functional participation strengthening interpersonal relationships.[2]

Neglected social dimensions can result in missed opportunities that can contribute to an inherent inability to capitalise on tacit knowledge, including hidden knowledge yet to be codified, expressed and shared.[3] Organisations effectively release and influence tacit knowledge[4] when they manage an often-neglected social dimension through team-building or social events such as get-togethers or staff parties.[5]

High-quality agential relationships are invaluable, not easily created and often challenging to imitate. Thus, an organisation's ability to encourage and facilitate interactions at different levels can be beneficial. [6] Agential tacit knowledge becomes useless in isolation,[7] which is why socialisation manifests useful opportunities to share such knowledge and transmit experience, skills and processes.[8] Further, socialisation provides opportunities to identify, rectify and build on knowledge deficiencies through a process of rapport, resonance and synchronisation.

In organisations with agents of diverse cultural backgrounds, different groups often interact in their native language with such distinct groups known as cliques, who casually share information with other members of the group.[9] Native language interaction can mean that socialisation processes result in less than total integration into the dominant–often Western–culture.[10] When organisations create structures that support and embrace groups and encourage greater cooperation, these cliques have the potential to be utilised to increase productivity.[11] Thus, managed socialisation as a process can create potential change opportunities,[12] which allow for the reconfiguration of organisational networks and relationships.

48. Agential Interactions

Organisational systems comprise of agents who can adapt to knowledge and creativity that result in opportunities for influence and leadership, which emerge through each interaction.[1] System-level self-organisation is essential for innovative outcomes within organisations.[2]

Complexity theory suggests that single agents are not responsible for uncontrolled complex interactions that occur during social processes.[3] Thus, power in social settings can transcend agentially and become systemic,[4] in which **leadership interprets from evolving experiences rather than from agential attributes**.[5] Interactions coexist finely or at the individual level, and coarsely or at the organisational level.[6] Reflexive and non-reflexive emergence result from agential interactions through boundaries, feedback and cohesion.[7] Reflexive emergence occurs through agential self-awareness, and conversely, non-reflexive emergence transpires through agential unawareness. Therefore, nonlinearity and unpredictability characterise communications when agents self-centre and self-actualise.[8] In organisations, agential interaction occurs in groups. Group interactions represent a complex adaptive system due to the influence they play on emergent behaviour[9] to generate unexpected outcomes[10] that result in innovation.[11]

Complexity refers to systems with disparate elements, which permit multiple configurations.[12] Such possibility highlights the criticality of interactions between different parts of complex systems and their behaviours, as any actions may have global effects.[13] Practical support with physical facilities encourages interactive activity[14] because the nature of interactions results in collective corporate intelligence.[15] Thus, complexity leadership facilitates a framework to understand emergent leadership,[16] which seeks to comprehend how self-organisation at a system-level emerges from agential interactions or nodes in organisations.[17]

A complex system view emphasises creative emergent outcomes through agential interaction at lower organisational levels.[18] Consequently, leadership becomes a collaborative activity in which agents situationally contribute to becoming leaders or followers as situations demand or permit.[19] Collaborative activity empowers agents to effectively fulfil their roles and improve collective and individual capacities,[20] also known as plural leadership.[21] Thus, further research is required to explore and understand how system-level self-organisation leads to innovation.[22] Agential interaction can organically generate creativity and innovation, which can assist and create a positive climate that encourages interaction. Agential interactions can, therefore, translate into increased innovation, creativity and a highly motivated, engaged social capital to result in competitive advantage and sustainability.

49. Interactions

The third aim of this book was to 'gain insights into how system-level self-organisation emerges from informal agential interaction.' Data analysis revealed the presence of adaptive leadership elements. However, these elements closely align with a cybernetic leadership focus, which suggests a leadership continuum within the organisation from cybernetic to adaptive leadership. As previously noted, interactions encourage conversations around topics of mutual interest, which in turn generate rapport and trust among the agents who associate. Consequently, in organisations, agents generally interact through different mediums such as face-to-face, email and instant messenger, and socialise at company-organised or private events.

Agential structural context partly determines interactions among agents within organisations,[1] which accelerate organisational knowledge flows.[2] Conversations are a critical source and medium through which such energy builds and transmits to keep systems and organisations in function.[3] Social interactions are organisationally tension susceptible, which affects where and how knowledge generates, accumulates, and consequently affects adaptation.[4] Innovation is an essential characteristic of such complex behaviour, which emerges when unexpected behavioural or structural change results in self-organisation.[5]

Stakeholder interactions generally remain the responsibility of agents accountable for their management at their level because they can foster these relationships. However, interactions at senior levels generally remains the responsibility of managers. In some cases, top-down communication can be problematic because management may withhold information and not interact at lower organisational levels. Thus, openness across all levels with free vertical and horizontal information flows can increase interactions in organisations because withholding information across departments produces organisational inefficiencies and knowledge gaps.

Interactivity reflects properties referred to as attractors, which exist fluidly, and are continuously in flux between formal or emergent leadership.[6] Interactions in complex, dynamic environments result in a continual evolving social structure that determines future associations to allow system-level adaptation and survival.[7] Interactions, influence and interdependent behaviours generate agential change where widespread value chain behavioural outcomes continuously feedback on one another, thus change effects become change causes.[8] Over time, agential convergence towards consensus requires dislodgement through an injection of different views[9] from external networks,[10] which can also help fill skills gaps and identify agents with the right skills.

This case study was a young organisation in which most of the original founder employees had exited the organisation voluntarily or through forced redundancies. Long-term agents have established relationships and networks that tend to consume higher interaction energy, which means that new agents can freely interact and nurture their own relationships and networks.[11] The assimilation of new agents in organisations can occur through social interactions that the organisation facilitates or be initiated by new entrants when they hold common interests with others. However, personally initiated interactions to build networks to understand the organisational culture, policies, procedures and production processes can result in a significant loss of interaction energy.

Multinational organisations have established networks and relationships that stem from one of the two main cultural groups. Where network nodes within cultural groups interact and communicate within their own social group, generally to the exclusion of the other dominant culture. In the interactions process, social groups exist, which enable agents from one dominant culture to build on and recreate sense and structures that appear culturally familiar to them, and in the process facilitate the creation of cultural silos. Consequently, homophily in organisations exhibits as the disposition of agents to connect with similar others, which limits knowledge distribution opportunities.[12]

Conversations in organisations help to develop rapport and trust, which is critical for knowledge distribution. Non work-related conversations or private interactions in the workplace also occur when agents want to grow personal friendships or enhance their chances of success in the organisation.[13] Organisations, therefore, need to increase interactions and socialisation to facilitate opportunities for agents to interact with a united organisation culture, which results in benefits associated with tightness among associations.[14] Tightness among associations makes the dissipation of energy in the form of information, ideas, or gossip accessible. Tightness will also push the system more quickly towards instability and facilitate opportunities to create a new order to the system,[15] which can give rise to creative adaptation and innovation.[16]

As previously discussed, managed socialisation manifests as a need to evaluate social interactions through a guided process and to understand and complete links to knowledge management.[17] Some organisations encourage social interactions through company-sponsored gym memberships and employee-run social clubs, which organise different social activities for employees. Interactions and socialisation provide deeper organisational awareness of behaviours and work styles. However, such opportunities need to be voluntary because forced interaction does not necessarily foster meaningful engagements and interactions. Additionally, personal situations with family and children dictate how much time agents can spend with colleagues after work because personal commitments can restrict social activities. Although some agents may not enjoy personal connections and will naturally limit interactions and how they build relationships, antisocial conduct does not generally stifle creativity and innovation.

50. Generative Relationships

Leadership seeks to foster and sustain generative and higher-quality relationships among agents in organisations,[1] which prevail when results remain uncertain. Consequently, adaptive leadership occurs as a dynamic that underlies emergent change inherent in generative leadership.[2] Generative leaders are outcome and solution-focused[3] and emphasise the efficient allocation of resources across multiple systems.

To facilitate the flow and speed of interactions within the organisation, generative leaders retain and reuse ideas created from activities. During the process, generative leaders increase the amount of information available for creativity to flourish.[4] To increase the idea generation pool in organisations, retention and reuse of ideas occurs through ideas distribution and brainstorming. However, to increase innovation and creativity, organisations need to establish processes or a dedicated department to collate, analyse and implement such ideas. Generative relationships among agents signify a means by which new contexts and characteristics, willingness to change and organisational structures that determine communication protocols emerge from mutual interests.[5] Generative relationships can also build mutual admiration to improve the quality of interactions with other stakeholders, which allows open and respectful conversations to take place.

When agential requirements remain inconsistent, their goals, behaviours and actions may conflict.[6] However, fundamental shared agential needs[7] become transparent with the emergence of self-organised groups. Self-organised groups allow the expression and fulfilment of covert drives, emotions, and desires.[8] Additionally, the application of Eastern philosophies of bingcun hubu or mutual coexistence[9] manages different cultures and can alleviate situations in which conflicts arise. For example, bingcun hubu can be a bridge between two dominant cultures because it integrates and forces them together to allow the organisation to capitalise on the generated synergies. The development of strong relationships can result in improved communication to assist and create innovative opportunities. However, the importance of ethnocultural diversity to create innovation requires further consideration.[10]

51. Networks

Engagement with the external mind critically allows organisations to tap into an internally lacking knowledge and skills base. Organisations regularly use reliable contractors and consultants because such transient groups have the required specialised skills. Organisations can, therefore, acquire knowledge from interactions with the external mind to utilise their knowledge, tools, expertise and networks, which can enhance or substitute capability.[1] Transient groups can assist in raising relationships between the organisational agents and external mind.

Organisations can foster agential networks, facilitate recreational scenarios and allow free agential interaction. Organisations can also provide a platform to encourage social communication and assist personal agential relationships, which integrate with professional interactions to extend organisational networks. However, sometimes organisations seek to tightly control when they facilitate such interactions which can be an invasion of privacy, especially when agents stay onsite on a FIFO rostered pattern. Site presence can hinder team-based interactions because not everyone can attend at the same time, which negatively affects departmental productivity through a feeling of being left out. Organisations can also facilitate socialisation through interactions and onsite functions around roster changeovers, which allow all agents to take part.

Workplace relationships of site-based agents spill over into their personal space when agents keep in touch and interact over their rostered breaks, which depends on and results from current rapport and relationships, with agents only able to see each other on changeover days. Agents can keep in touch and engage with departed colleagues, which constitutes an engagement with the external mind. However, interactions and relationships remain about like-minded people who enjoy each other's company and want to interact outside of the workplace.[2] For organisations, tension and challenges exist to determine the balance between an environment in which relationships develop and flourish and ensuring the organisation does not impinge on agential free time.

52. Communication

Through agential interactions, organisations can understand how leadership functions and manifests, and in the process foster creativity, influence and positive change,[1] which results in the emergence of adaptive leadership. When efforts, negotiations, communications and adjustments are uncontrolled or unknown, organisations become predictable from ongoing agential interactions because these interactions have bottom-up properties that remain uncomprehended or unpredicted:[2]

These interactions have a bottom up quality[3] which no one fully understands or is able to fully predict the outcome of.[4]

The future of organisations in dynamic environments relies on accelerated pattern configurations[5] in which active nonlinear agential interactions occur,[6] and facilitate a rapid response to unexpected challenges.[7] In the complex systems view, organisations exist as social networks which comprise adaptive agents who resonate when they express mutual interests, knowledge and goals based on their interaction activity.[8] Organisational agents include agents from the environment[9] who network with the external mind. Emergent leadership often shapes through delicate but intricate dynamic interactions between these networked agents.[10] Organically generated creativity has a bearing on organisational innovativeness and makes it easier to integrate knowledge from the external mind.[11]

Effective organisational communication is critical with a highly diverse workforce because disparate agential views require consideration to foster creativity and innovation.[12] Organisations in the natural resource sector generally have production site offices as well as geographically dispersed head offices. Consequently, communication intensity and effectiveness lead to collaborations with and among agents at different geographical locations, which can generate innovative capability and organisational success.[13]

A focus on effective communication through agential interactions offers a leadership model in which organisations can easily explore complex issues.[14] Organisations operate as complex systems, with fluid arrays of desired conditions or objectives that partially diverge.[15] Simulations of CASs emphasise the correlation characteristics of complexity, and discuss, highlight four elements of such complex systems[16] which facilitate and nurture generative relationships[17] to yield new knowledge significant for innovation,[18] and consequently organisational sustainability as well as a competitive advantage:

1. Organisational outcomes emerge from agential interaction at lower levels.[19]

2. Self-organisation in systems emerges from interdependent agential behaviour and local information.[20] Rarely explained through simple cause–effect mechanisms,[21] these interactions are nonlinear.[22]

3. Nonlinear interaction also results in the emergence of dynamic and non-static processes and structures.[23]

4. Over time, complex systems emerge and evolve through

agential configuration and change.[24] Due to nonlinearity, these systems unpredictably change to create amplified outcomes and become increasingly complex.[25] Multinational organisations with a transient workforce operate in such dynamic environments, which continually transform through the entry and exit of agents.

Typically volatile and fundamental to knowledge creation, creativity has unpredictable outcomes that exhibit in different states.[26] Therefore, organisations that exploit relational networks as a source of knowledge and collaborative approach have better chances to innovate.[27] The exploitation of relation networks fosters creativity and generates innovative solutions from the external mind[28] and informal agential interaction. However, 'unless people believe that they can produce desired effects by their actions, they have little incentive to act or to persevere in the face of difficulty.'[29]

Leaders must communicate with certainty, capably handle any environmental obstacles, and instil confidence.[30] Additionally, effective leaders must project confidence, strength, authority, listening skills, broad experience, authenticity, and an ability to inspire followers. Such qualities aid effortless communication as leaders possess the necessary knowledge and awareness.

Communication remains a primary means to regenerate structure, which requires the combination of information, utterances and awareness that exist independently from the system,[31] resulting in 'autopoiesis'.[32] Autopoiesis occurs when agents experience themselves as independent beings while contributing to the identity and experiences of others within the environment.[33] In multicultural organisations, thin communication is the principal cause of frustration, which alleviates when organisations dictate that all written correspondence be in English or accompanied by a translation. Conveying the importance of dialogue in English allows all agents to understand corporate communication and fosters creativity and innovation.

53. Thin Communication

Non-professional speakers of English remain partially restricted to a smaller range of vocabulary, which facilitates exchanges in business settings but limits talk and social exchange.[1] Thus, non-professional English speakers often fear that their lack of language skills may negatively reflect on how others perceive their professional knowledge and skills.[2] Interpretation can result in a loss of meaning, which depends on the context.[3] Consequently, in multicultural organisational settings, non-native English speakers may interpret knowledge differently from native English speakers. Thus, a difference in interpretation results in a recurrent alteration of meaning as knowledge disperses within the organisation.[4]

Emergent leaders use language and consider broader views to understand organisational direction and thereby gain clarity when agents convey a consistent message.[5] However, in multicultural organisations, the predominance of multiple languages and communication mediums makes this challenging. Thus, organisations can instil the importance of English communication as a shared language. The prevalence and reluctance of non-English speakers to converse, communicate, write or provide feedback in English can generate frustration and annoyance among the English speakers as they cannot read or understand the non-English communication without translation.

English speakers may also find non-English communication disrespectful and not understand why it remains widely practised in predominantly Western organisations. Presumably, non-English speakers experience similar difficulties with communication in English. Thus, such frustration generates constant tension between these two groups, with a familiar language and context creation from a non-familiar language. However, the intricacies of communication problems between locals and Western expatriates in multinational organisations is yet to be widely understood and analysed.[6]

Culture affects agential engagement and can result in creative and innovative behaviours. These can benefit organisations considerably, although too much control over after-hours interactions can ultimately hinder creativity and innovation. After-hours agential interactions can be encouraged through subsidised gym memberships and social clubs that hold regular social events. Such interplays support accountability, for instance, agents can inquire about missed gym sessions or social events in effect conducting a welfare check.

Ensure agential participation and interaction, particularly in team-building activities, remains an integral part of managerial roles. While the participation rate in company events usually remains below 100 per cent, organisations cannot discount the importance of such events to build trust and awareness. Personal level awareness in which agents interact through managed events can allow them to build trust, understand likes, dislikes and interests of others as well as support these friendships to transpose easily into daily work interactions. Additionally, significant interactions can occur when agents value their time spent together.

Onsite-facilitated interactions can create concerns, as a two weeks presence onsite with an inherent inability to cope with other agents can be very difficult. Team-building activities might benefit organisations because leadership generally emerges from lower levels, which allows the organisation to identify potential. However, team functions onsite can be a challenge to host as it can affect production and staff safety with the risk of intoxicated agents on the job from alcohol that organisations may provide. Sometimes, social network promotion and managed socialisation remain a foreign ideology to some management who do not see any value to the organisation, and hence do not encourage these.

Agential interactions remain a vital source to share information, ideas and problems to develop solutions. However, although integral to each role, agential complacency restricts creative thought processes and continuous improvement. Thus, it becomes essential to continually acknowledge team concerns and organisational objectives. Additionally, teams function better and more productively from such combined collaboration when agents persist and get involved in interactions to benefit the organisation. Open discussions from collaboration and combined interactivity encourage the sharing of thoughts, and support agents to modify and improve on combined team thoughts and ideas to collectively become team ideas.

Task performance requires openness, which permits organisations to incorporate diverse views and take risks. Openness can develop into robust agential relationships with a higher degree of honesty and trust. These relationships facilitate communication and allow agents organisational access across levels to share ideas. Organisations can thereby take decision responsibility and make informed decisions based on complete information from all organisational levels. Openness also enables and empowers agents to understand the role requirements and perform. Further, relationships and agential role swaps can be a means to cross-skill and share the knowledge that provides an inclusive functional understanding and support to answer queries or handle challenges within organisations.

General agential conversations help to facilitate rapport and build relationships between agents, without such connections and interactions, agents may feel uncomfortable to work with each other. Regular communication also assists in teaching and acquiring knowledge from agents. Discussions and interactions help to understand other agents, their work ethic, build respect, provide open conversation channels and generally collaborate better.

Full handover of tasks between staff can assist organisations to retain knowledge, for example, sharing document processes, procedures and the storage of documentation in designated locations for complete staff access. In dynamic environments, this also assists in change adaptability as it requires a flexible team able to share ideas as well as apply acquired prior knowledge efficiently and effectively. Cross-level meetings is another means which allows agents from lower levels to present their ideas as such ideas can highlight previously unconsidered problems by management. These sessions provide an overall perspective on current organisational issues. Conversely, managers who fixate on predetermined outcomes use a blinkered approach, which effectively discounts or disregards divergent ideas and consequently hinders creativity and innovation.

Industry user groups and conferences can be useful to keep abreast of industry developments, with much innovation occurring in the public and private sector that can benefit the organisation. Groups promote knowledge sharing and can result in organisational connections and relationships that facilitate processes instead of the withholding of knowledge. Networking with past peers and employees also allow organisations to secure and employ people with the right skills because they can easily use networks to validate candidate work history.

54. Essentialism

Organisations can acquire, distribute and communicate culture,[1] which results from and induces social interaction. Contextual judgement is central to the misrepresentation of agential expectations or beliefs,[2] which help in judging their interests and actions. Such views fundamentally link to the culture that[3] agents hold about expectations other agents have of them.[4] Thus, essentialism manifests as a tendency to assign a fixed or static quality to the cultural differences of an entire group to which an individual belongs.[5] Essentialism or 'reification',[6] overstate the importance of group features to misrepresent the perception of a whole group.[7]

Agential interactions socially create certainty within organisations through negotiation and the awareness of individual experiences.[8] Reality and culture construct through interactions when such organisational contexts undergo constant deconstruction and reconstruction as agents create reality and sense from information available to them. However, social interaction as a Western ideology is usually an unnecessary distraction from a non-Western perspective. In multicultural organisations, essentialism of different cultural backgrounds of management can prevail, with a possibility of negative performance bias towards different culture managers. Although, organisational tenure can decrease friction and the degree to which cultural diversity negatively influences performance. Essentialism can lead to conflicts through cultural stereotypes, which is essential for cultural integration and effective communication to evolve the business through cultural synergies.

Adaptive challenges occur as organisational problems with solutions that originate from agents, which alter the values, beliefs, assumptions and behaviours of people and their work.[9] However, a lack of transparency and communication from upper management can affect decisions made within organisations. Numerous challenges faced by multicultural organisations result from diverse cultural, communication and management styles, which conflict with the Western style. Therefore, to understand how individual departments and teams effectively collaborate, organisations require consistency in information and flexibility to make changes dynamically to address these challenges.

Part Eight: Adaptive Leadership

Adaptive leadership occurs as an interactive event in which knowledge, action preferences and behaviours change to provoke an organisation to become increasingly adaptive.[1] In this process, organisational knowledge transfer is likely to occur among interconnected employees,[2] with **identity and tension** as the two main drivers of adaptive leadership.[3] Consequently, a new identity forms over time when agents mutually interact to define social identities and change how the current rules govern them. A unique social identity defines when agents envision issues that require new knowledge, innovation or behaviour, and they engage proactively or reactively in interactive behaviour to address these challenges.[4] As living organisms, organisations share an identity and purpose[5] requiring open, honest and harmonious relationships among agents. Additionally, fundamental assumptions form the foundation of complex systems, which highlight that organisational problems are complex and generally unsolvable through rational thought.[6] Operational conditions further dictate satisfaction rather than optimisation and thus, organisations generally generate suboptimal solutions to complex problems.[7]

Organisations trigger flexibility through changes in knowledge, actions and behaviours when they tackle challenges[8] that exist systemically and affect long-term feasibility, which demands creative thinking and changes in agential behaviour. Consequently, agential tacit awareness and skills contain solutions to systemic difficulties.[9] Such challenges also require new know-how, discoveries and operating modes, which make them non-compliant with standard procedures or leadership orders.[10] A fundamental insight of adaptive leadership recognises the relational nature of interactions and their importance for organisational change, which results in nonlinear adaptive outcomes through a process of research, exploration and adaptation from agential interactions.[11]

Agential interactions highlight the essence of relationships[12] where we can only understand human nature through a mutual connection between distinct individuals.[13] Further, relationships or organisational changes specifically emerge from the space between individuals, which highlights that the self and the other in interactions remain inseparable.[14] Inseparability, thus, results in an enquiry into the essence of interactions and relationships that occur within organisations.[15]

Administrative, adaptive and enabling are functions that describe complex systems leadership, with the enabling component bridging the administrative and adaptive functions. Administrative focuses on organisational issues, whereas adaptive manifests through agents who voluntarily and informally interact to generate emergent productive outcomes through mutual dependency, resulting in adaptive leadership.[16]

Adaptive leadership is a collaborative experience which transforms agential knowledge, actions and behaviours[17] that encourage and mobilise agents to handle harsh challenges, flourish and routinely perform beyond their formal job descriptions.[18] Consequently, adaptive leadership results in functional participation that organisations rely upon to operate effectively.[19]

Identity and tension occur as principal drivers of adaptive leadership where a combined social identity forms through the tension between mutually interacting agents to change how current rules govern them.[20] A combined social identity exhibits through proactive or reactive engagement in interactive behaviours as agents envision organisational issues that require creativity, innovation or behavioural change, and address these challenges.[21] In the interactive process, agents may experience tension from contradicting views that challenge and force changes in their understanding of current issues to accommodate new possibilities that alleviate the conflict.[22] Thus, adaptive leadership manifests when innovation and positive change emerge from such tension.[23]

However, due to a prevalence of transient social capital and an increase in the use of outsourced contractors and consultants in the resources sector, over time social identity is a challenge to establish because social capital reflects the presence of direct and personal relationships among individuals within organisations. Recognising the influence of adaptive leadership can assist and introduce strategies that retain social capital and limit the decay of collective corporate intelligence because in a knowledge economy, talent attraction and retention persist more significantly than downsizing and restructuring.[24]

55. Innovation

The essence of innovation is to re-create the world according to a particular vision or ideal.[1]

Product innovation can either be radical, involving total transformation,[2] or incremental, in which modifications and refinements occur through a process of continuous improvement.[3] A shortage of labour, other resources, and the lack of a dedicated team to analyse ideas can limit radical or incremental improvement activity. In this case study, agential initiatives and positive collaboration on ideas that facilitated knowledge distribution and encouragement within forums fostered innovation. Organic knowledge generation results from the dedication of specific resources to knowledge processes, which is one of the most effective methods to encourage employees to be creative and innovative. [4] Consequently, despite the need to work efficiently and effectively, agential negativity can easily set in with the lack of organisational resources.

Knowledge can generate from employee self-development or corporate training regimes. Training and development investments correlate with a variety of personal and organisational benefits in which the development of agential skills hinge on broader business objectives.[5] At an agential level, training investment constitutes a powerful signal that reassures agents that their contribution is valued by the organisation, which increases agential motivation and commitment to overall objectives.[6] Agential encouragement is crucial to share and develop individual learning into collective corporate intelligence,[7] with the ability to learn faster than competitors the only sustainable organisational competitive advantage.[8] Organisations can facilitate opportunities for agents to learn about innovation through workshops. Additionally, organisations should gain a thorough knowledge of agential capabilities to provide them with suitable challenges.

Within the resource sector, innovation commonly occurs when an organisation runs into resource limitations, which limits opportunities for innovation to continuous improvement:

> *"Not a lot of people are going to be doing innovation, because they don't need to... The guys don't even have to get up and look out their window and they already have $4 billion of work going on in the area. So, why innovate?[9]"*

Resource limitations point to tension, with a lack of incentive to innovate in boom times and the high risk of innovation during downtimes.

56. Attractors

Attractor dynamics are relevant to individual and social processes, which can assist and simplify the interpretation of systems dynamics through the construction of diverse social-psychological experiences.[1] The thoughts, attitudes and behaviours of individuals also tend to converge towards relatively narrow sets of patterns or states–known as attractors–which they support to maintain and return to relatively quickly despite external destabilising forces.[2] Similar to gravitational fields, attractors pull behaviours towards them with four different types:

1. strange,
2. oscillating,
3. quasi and
4. fixed-point.

Strange attractors are non-repeating, predictable and stable in the short-term but unpredictable and unstable in the longer term,[3] which results from 'nonlinearity and interactivity'.[4] Oscillating attractors fluctuate between stability and instability,[5] while quasi-attractors are unstable.[6] Fixed-point attractors are associated with rigidity and stability within organisations,[7] and due to lower dynamics increasingly common in poorly performing teams.[8]

The initial belief or state of an attractor is known as its 'basin of attraction.' Consequently, reversible changes correspond to shifts between attractors, whereas non-reversible changes correspond to structural alterations in attractors.[9] The basin of attraction for organisational agents relates to the cultural, social, professional and personal belief systems that they uphold, and which the agents tend to fall back on in times of uncertainty.[10] Thus, in multicultural organisations there are often two or more concurrent national and organisational cultures, so agents frequently seek stability for what they understand and fall back onto familiar languages or modes of operation.

Intrinsic positive attractors define system states and comprise a broad basin of attraction. Intrinsic positive attractors swiftly dislodge conflict and force a system to gravitate towards equilibrium or convergence to a new basin of attraction.[11] Rewards motivate agents to be creative or voice improvement opportunities, conversely, absence of tangible rewards results in creative activity disengagement. Thus, material rewards mirror oscillating-attractors, as the provision of rewards is perceived to induce stability and foster creativity.

Fixed-point attractors persist as the simplest types of attractors that lead to a stable desired 'end state'.[12] When organisations advise agents of an end state but then provide them with accountability and freedom, agents have the flexibility to determine optimum solutions and to attain such an end state.

57. Identity and Tension

Although uncomfortable, agents positively respond to stress that arises from interdependencies and interactions to generate new knowledge, capabilities, innovation and adaptability.[1] Tension produces transformation at the organisational level, thus making it an asset that requires continual encouragement.[2]

In multicultural organisations, leadership issues around the cultural identity of the organisations and their agents exist, with foreign ownership resulting in an expatriate senior management leadership culture. Thus, a lack of vision, key objectives and how management encourages lower organisational levels to embrace these can create tension at lower agential levels within organisations. There are other areas of tension that dampen creativity and innovation in organisations, summarised at the end of this chapter. However, some stress remains necessary to facilitate creativity and innovation, with the challenge being to ensure there is a balance between these two forces.

58. Resonate

Through interactions agents resonate, dissipate energy and amplify organisational competencies.[1] Thus, interactions influence the tendency in organisations to self-organise,[2] which leads to relationships and the fostering of adaptive tension.[3] Creative outcomes resonate with group needs and experience as well as group acceptance that provides creative workers with validation.[4] Further, when guided by a genial motivation for other agential perspectives, agents direct their natural motivation to produce novel and useful ideas, which achieves higher creativity.[5]

Having a dedicated business improvement department to collate and analyse the benefit of new ideas becomes a necessity in organisations. Such a department provides focus and an avenue for creativity and innovation to nurture and be recognised, with its absence viewed as detrimental to innovation generation. A centralised department can provide alignment across different departments in the organisation as there may be similar issues elsewhere, as well as overcome and dissemble silos. The lack of a dedicated department reflects an example of social capital erosion, with many lost opportunities to capitalise on internally generated creativity and innovation.

Correlation relates to the awareness that emerges in social system interactions, motivated through mutual unrecognised human needs and desires. [6] Correlation stands as one of the central mechanisms for creativity in which agents interact to share their preferences, thoughts, ideas and assumptions, which lead to resonance and creation of an 'attractor pit'.[7] Centres of excellence can create attractor pits to facilitate interactions with others and are central to the creative and innovative process. Because agents spend a significant amount of time at work, organisations need to openly and honestly relate with them to reduce stress and bitterness. Increasingly, working onsite as part of a couple in a relationship also creates work stability because couples can provide any necessary mutual support. Previous close work relationships can also help build productive relationships. Consequently, agential resonance in some organisations occurs as an accidental consequence rather than the result of a purposeful organisational strategy.

59. Summary

Creativity is essential throughout organisational structures and should be the responsibility of each agent, with creative solutions generated through continuous improvement or incremental processes highlighting how innovation is often employee driven. Conversely, an absence of recognition or reward discourages creativity and innovation, thus, organisations must recognise that balance is required to foster creativity.

The collation, assessment, reward and application of ideas that manifest creativity and innovation serve to drive innovation critical motivation within organisations. Organisations need to address a lack of resources, recognition, reward and requirement because quality systems nurture organisational creativity and innovation. Further, trust, resonance and fear are also elements that can either foster or hinder creativity and innovation.

This chapter highlights four critical gaps to address organisational constraints in the research literature:

1. Knowledge retention addresses the leakage of knowledge through the exit of long-tenured knowledge workers from the organisation.[1]
2. The importance of clear communication between locals and expatriates in multinational organisations.[2]
3. The impact of ethno-cultural diversity to create innovative opportunities within organisations.[3]
4. The importance and value of agential voices within organisations.[4]

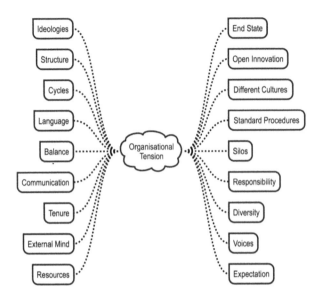

Figure 8.1: Organisational Tension Identified

The following list presents key findings concerning areas of stress and tension that **dampen creativity and innovation** in organisations, with key terms underlined to clearly identify links with objectives:

1. Utilise the mission command philosophy to arrive at the end state.

2. Use consultants to support open innovation and reliance on competitors.

3. Create and nurture rich connections across distinctly different cultures.

4. Follow <u>standard procedures</u> against the need to find new solutions.

5. <u>Silos</u> discourage knowledge distribution and result in learned helplessness.

6. Stress between ownership or <u>responsibility</u> and the requirement to adhere to standard operational procedures.

7. Stress due to <u>diversity</u> within teams and in cross-functional teams.

8. Tension from lack of tangible recognition, which silences agential <u>voices</u>.

9. Lack of clarity about role <u>expectations</u> and additional contributions to creativity and innovation.

10. Stress through lack of funds and dedicated organisational <u>resources</u>.

11. Tension from the application of different management <u>ideologies</u>.

12. The need to consider ideas from across levels against an organisational <u>structure</u> that discounts these ideas.

13. Stress created through boom and bust <u>cycles,</u> which impacts on investment in creativity and innovation.

14. Tension that arises in diverse cultural groups from <u>language</u> differences.

15. Tension and challenges to determine a <u>balance</u> that encourages an environment in which relationships develop and flourish.

16. Stress from the absence of internal <u>structure</u>.

17. Tension from a lack of <u>communication</u> regarding organisational strategies.

18. Tension between the need to increase social capital and manage <u>tenure</u> within organisations.

19. Stress because the <u>external mind</u> retains knowledge and skills that relate to innovation.

20. Tension due to the need for <u>resources</u> to foster creativity and innovation and a lack of labour and abilities to perform day-to-day activities.

Stress and tension are used interchangeably throughout this book and occur as one of the two main drivers of adaptive leadership with the areas of tension experienced summarised in Figure 8.1. Organisations can address these areas of tension and consequently, become increasingly creative and innovative.

A model also emerges containing features and elements that enable or impede adaptive leadership to influence intellectual capital management in which organisations encourage, facilitate and influence social capital, creativity and innovation. Tension remains a critical driver for adaptive leadership because it dampens creativity and innovation. The intensity needed to foster creativity and innovation and how this balances against stress that sustains equilibrium is also highlighted. Organisations, therefore, need to ensure adaptive leadership provides a context for creativity and innovation.

Consequently, Figure 8.2 proposes a model that emerges from the findings of this case study. This model reflects a need for a structural space that organisations can facilitate to address some areas of tension illustrated in Figure 8.1.

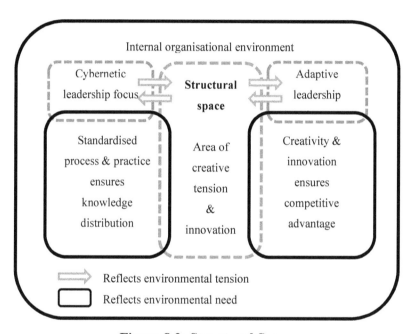

Figure 8.2: Structural Space

In the area of creative tension and innovation, structural space emerges as a consequence of tension between preserving a cybernetic leadership focus against the requirement to be creative and innovative by applying an adaptive leadership focus. In organisational contexts, structural space is then the equilibrium between the necessity for standardisation and the demand for creativity and innovation. The arrows within Figure 8.2 show areas of tension in the internal organisational environment, highlighted in Figure 8.1. These areas of tension reflect persistent oscillations between two leadership styles and focal points. Thus, structural space becomes an attractor pit, where attention gravitates, dislodges and shifts with the force and energy of tension.

60. Opportunities for Research

Technological advances and economic globalisation have resulted in uncertainty and turbulence in the postmodern knowledge economy which has resulted in continuous dynamic change, challenges and diminished productivity,[1] with organisations viewed as intricate, interconnected, emotional and turbulent.[2]

Gaps identified from a review of current academic research highlight issues that affect organisational sustainability, which propose that a clear link exists between aspects of complexity leadership theory and intellectual capital management. Several questions arise, such as:

- how does complexity leadership influence innovation and know-how,[3]
- what influences social capital creation,[4]
- how does innovation emerge from system-level self-organisation,[5]
- what sustains relationships between interactions, knowledge

processes and competitive advantage,[6]

- what influences various mechanisms and how can they be measured,[7]

- what are the requirements to articulate social interactions as processes, how are these processes essential to manage knowledge[8] and

- how do the different properties of knowledge management challenges in global organisations impact organisational life?[9]

The following chapter concludes and discusses the contributions of this book, highlights limitations and areas of future research.

Part Nine: Conclusion

61. Theoretical Application

The motivation and inspiration behind the study which formed the basis of this book were to understand:

> **'How can Adaptive Leadership leverage on intellectual capital management to positively impact on social capital, creativity and innovation?'**

Part Eight highlights areas that generate stress and inhibit creativity and innovation. Tension manifests in organisations from standardised processes, practices to assure knowledge distribution and the need for creativity and innovation, which ensures competitive advantage.

The necessity for standardisation manifests from a cybernetic leadership approach, as discussed in Part Three. Conventional views of leadership have a cybernetic focus that actions of leaders appear to reflect in an attempt to control organisational behaviour to achieve specific results. Therefore, leaders constrain self-organisation emergence as divergent and in need of control and rectification.[1] Constraining self-organisation emergence is consistent with a transactional leadership style,[2] which manifests in most organisations.

In cybernetic leadership, leaders focus on the external environment to make choices and select operational strategies that result in predictable outcomes for the organisation.[3] Thus, cybernetic leadership emphasises the skills agents possess to assist organisations achieve organisational goals. Cybernetic leaders also use relationships as a power source for action in the organisation and are aware of the interactional effects and reactions that result from these relationships.[4] Further, cybernetic leaders use appropriate transactions to motivate agential behaviours as leaders desire.[5]

Conversely, a focus on adaptive leadership suggests the need for creativity and innovation to ensure competitive advantage, as discussed in Part Eight. Adaptive leadership occurs as a collaborative experience through which organisational awareness, actions and behaviours transform to catalyse organisations to become adaptive.[6] Adaptive leadership also encourages and mobilises staff to handle harsh challenges, flourish and routinely perform beyond their formal job descriptions,[7] which results in functional participation that organisations can rely on for effective operations.[8] An adaptive leadership approach emphasises workplace agential skills and their capacity to assist the organisation to realise creative and innovative–although perhaps less predictable–solutions.

Research suggests that organisations benefit when they facilitate and enable social interactions within organisations. Thus, the importance of organisational structures and structural spaces to facilitate the generation of ideas and develop collaboration is crucial. Sometimes, the capacity of an organisation to enable changes to increase interactions through some of its practices occurs unintentionally. For example, a focus on physical space constraints imposed in work environments appears to be significant. For instance, the contraction of floor space of one organisation encouraged interactions, helped break apart a silo culture, although in some areas different silos may have emerged. The facilitation and enablement of social interactions within organisations corresponds with Moitra and Kumar's (2007)[9] view on managed socialisation.

An independent department such as an excellence centre,[10] or a research and development department[11] are organisational structural elements that facilitate creativity and innovation, including opportunities for the collation, analysis, deployment, implementation and reward of innovative ideas. The advantage of a dedicated department structure also facilitates and provides social status to creativity and innovation within the organisation.

A second structural feature is a business improvement department, which can play a highly symbolic role in organisations. The business improvement department's visibility across all levels of the organisation helps to dismantle existing silo cultures. The business improvement department can foster relationships as well as encourage and reward creativity and innovation in organisations. The lack of business improvement departments acts as a demotivating factor which creates a lack of direction, limits agents from creativity and identification of opportunities for improvement. Other research on excellence centres,[12] units of purpose[13] and the fostering of adaptive processes such as research and development[14] support the benefit of knowledge creation and retention.

As a further enabler of social interactions, the use of a common language for communication averts problems of essentialism and thin communication, which can arise between two or more distinct cultural groups within an organisation. Relational practices and organisational structures that encourage and recognise social interactions foster creativity and innovation. The recruitment and retention of employees with appropriate skills and experience also appear to assist the organisation in becoming increasingly creative and innovative.

This book has suggested that theories and research on adaptive leadership can benefit from a specific focus on aspects of organisational life that have little to do with formal objectives and predictable outcomes. The explicit recognition and fostering of social interactions, organisational structures and individual skills can cultivate an environment of creativity and culture, which can better adapt to unexpected external constraints than a cybernetic approach.

62. Practical Application

Acknowledging the demand for organisations to nurture and sustain structural space (see Figure 8.2) for creativity and innovation to thrive is a significant contribution to practice. An area of creative tension and innovation emerges from the stress that arises by preserving a cybernetic leadership focus against the requirement to be creative and innovative by applying an adaptive leadership focus. Organisations must, therefore, decrease barriers and intensify enabling factors to maximise the likelihood of structural space to emerge.

Appropriate knowledge management practices also help build on tacit knowledge and become foundational structures, as agents use tacit knowledge to wield power. Tacit knowledge supports creativity and innovation when organisations facilitate knowledge distribution and break apart silos and knowledge strongholds. For example, excellence centres encourage interactions and pool expert knowledge, which stands out as a strategy that the organisation can implement to enable innovation and creativity.

Management and increased agential interactions and socialisation to foster relationships and facilitate these connections are further strategies the organisation can consider. Silo cultures arising from two concurrent national and organisational cultures also create frustration and tension. Thus, organisations can provide supportive infrastructure and processes to foster creativity and innovation that aim to break apart silo cultures. Multinational organisations require clear communication policies that allow everyone to understand conveyed messages.

The lack of recognition and reward of innovative ideas remains a criticism of some organisations because it dampens the flow of creative ideas. Therefore, better systems for recognition and reward are required as well as specific resources to facilitate and foster creativity and innovation. Such steps will help organisations initiate a structural space and encourage innovation and creativity to flourish at all levels.

63. Limitations

The following considerations, outside the scope of this study and book, provide opportunities for potential future research:

1. Detailed analysis of reward, work engagement and needs theory to increase creativity and innovation.

2. Examination of personality types and their effects on creativity and innovation.

3. Dimensions of social culture with potential gaps in the culture and context of organisations, which direct awareness towards conscious cultural change and alignment to current organisational mindsets.

4. Communication concerns that arise between two or more distinct cultural groups.[1]

5. Relationships between interactions, knowledge processes and competitive advantage.[2]

6. The effects of, and how to measure various mechanisms.[3]

7. Enablers of social interactions and how organisations can establish and articulate this process as an essential component for knowledge management.[4]

8. Challenges of different aspects of knowledge management within global businesses and the effects on organisational life.[5]

Finally, apply the recommendations from this book in larger organisations, different industry sectors and other global environments to determine whether results are generalisable.

Notes and References

Introduction

1   Dicken, Peter. 2015. *Global shift: Mapping the changing contours of the world economy.* 7 ed The Guilford Press, New York, NY.,118.
2   D'Aveni, Richard A. 2010. *Hypercompetition: Managing the Dynamics of Strategic Manoeuvring.* NY: Simon and Schuster Inc.,2.
3   D'Aveni, Richard A. 1995. 'Coping with Hypercompetition: Utilizing the New 7S's Framework'. *Academy of Management Perspectives* 9 (3): 45–57. https://doi.org/10.5465/ame.1995.9509210281.

Part One: Challenge

1   Overview

1   Verma, Neena, and Anil Anand Pathak. 2011. 'Using Appreciative Intelligence for Ice-breaking: A New Design'. *Journal of Workplace Learning* 23 (4): 276–85; Wysocki Jr, B. 2000. 'Yet Another Hazard of the New Economy: The Pied Piper Effect'. *Wall Street Journal* 30 (3): 30.
2   Massingham, Peter. 2008. 'Measuring the Impact of Knowledge Loss: More Than Ripples on a Pond?' *Management Learning* 39 (5): 541–60.
3   Hatch, Mary Jo, and Ann L Cunliffe. 2013. *Organization Theory.* Third. Oxford University Press.

2   Background

1   Australian Bureau of Statistics. 2002. 'The Resources Industry in Western Australia'. 1367.5. Canberra, A.C.T: ABS.
2   Phillips, Ken. 2008. 'How the Government and Unions Help Maintain Australia's Skills Shortage'. *Institute of Public Affairs Review: A Quarterly Review of Politics and Public Affairs, The* 60 (1): 16–19.; Mineral Council of Australia. 2012. 'Submission to the Review of the Standards for the Regulation of Vocational Education and Training'. Mineral Council of Australia. http://www.minerals.org.au
3   Drucker, Peter F. 2003. 'New Trends in Management'. *Executive Excellence* 20 (8): 8–8.
4   Davenport, Thomas H. 2005. *Thinking for a Living: How to Get Better Performances And Results from Knowledge Workers.* Harvard Business

Press.
5   Miller, JW. 2011. 'The $200,000 a Year Mine Worker'. *Wall Street Journal* 16: B1.
6   Mineral Council of Australia. 2015. 'The Whole Story: New Publication Details Mining's Contribution to the Australian Community'. Mineral Council of Australia.
7   Mineral Council of Australia. 2014. 'Annual Report'. Mineral Council of Australia. http://www.minerals.org.au.
8   Mineral Council of Australia. 2012. 'Submission to the', 2.
9   Ibid, 3.
10   Drucker, Peter F. 2007. *The Effective Executive*. Butterworth-Heinemann, 4.
11   Starovic, Danka, and Bernard Marr. 2003. 'Understanding Corporate Value: Managing and Reporting Intellectual Capital', May, 1–28. www.cimaglobal.com.
12   Bolino, Mark C, William H Turnley, and James M Bloodgood. 2002. 'Citizenship Behavior and the Creation of Social Capital in Organisations'. *Academy of Management Journal* 27 (4): 505–22. http://www.medwelljournals.com.;Nasir, Rohany, MS Mohammadi, Wan Sulaiman Wan Shahrazad, Omar Fatimah, Rozainee Khairudin, and Fatimah Halim. 2011. 'Relationship between Organizational Citizenship Behavior and Task Performance'. *The Social Sciences* 6 (4): 307–312. http://www.medwelljournals.com.
13   Lee-Kelley, Liz, Deborah A. Blackman, and Jeffrey Peter Hurst. 2007. 'An Exploration of the Relationship between Learning Organisations and the Retention of Knowledge Workers'. *The Learning Organization* 14 (3): 204–21;Linderman, Albert, Daniel Pesut, and Joanne Disch. 2015. 'Sense Making and Knowledge Transfer: Capturing the Knowledge and Wisdom of Nursing Leaders'. *Journal of Professional Nursing* 31 (4): 290–97. https://doi.org/10.1016/j.profnurs.2015.02.004.
14   Alvesson, Mats. 2012. *Understanding Organizational Culture*. 2nd ed. SAGE.,8; Collins, James Charles, Jim Collins, and Jerry I. Porras. 2005. *Built to Last: Successful Habits of Visionary Companies*. Random House.,71.
15   Hiltrop, Jean-Marie. 1995. 'The Changing Psychological Contract: The Human Resource Challenge of the 1990s'. *European Management Journal* 13 (3): 286–94. https://doi.org/10.1016/0263-2373(95)00019-H.;Presti,

Alessandro Lo, and Sara Pluviano. 2016. 'Looking for a Route in Turbulent Waters: Employability as a Compass for Career Success'. *Organizational Psychology Review* 6 (2): 192–211.

16 Drucker, Peter F. 1999. 'Knowledge-Worker Productivity: The Biggest Challenge'. *California Management Review* 41 (2).

17 Drucker 2003. 'New Trends'.

18 Lee-Kelley, Blackman, and Hurst. 2007. 'An Exploration of'.

19 Phillips 2008. 'How the Government'; Mineral Council of Australia. 2012. 'Submission to the'.

20 Kalkan, Veli Denizhan. 2008. 'An Overall View of Knowledge Management Challenges for Global Business'. *Business Process Management Journal* 14 (3): 390–400.

21 Zack, Michael H. 1999. 'Managing Codified Knowledge'. *Sloan Management Review* 40 (4): 45–58.

22 Pfeffer, Jeffrey, and Robert I. Sutton. 2000. *The Knowing-Doing Gap: How Smart Companies Turn Knowledge Into Action*. Harvard Business Press, 256.

23 Barney, Jay B. 1991. 'Firm Resources and Sustained Competitive Advantage'. *Journal of Management* 17 (1): 99–120.; Collis, David J., and Cynthia A. Montgomery. 1995.'Competing on Resources: Strategy in the 1990s'. *Harvard Business Review* July-August: 119–28.; Paulraj, Antony. 2011.'Understanding the Relationships between Internal Resources and Capabilities, Sustainable Supply Management and Organizational Sustainability'. *Journal of Supply Chain Management* 47 (1): 19–37.; Porter, Michael E. 1985. *Competitive Advantage: Creating and Sustaining Superior Performance*. New York: The Free Press; A Division of Macmillan Inc.

24 Ibid

25 Zack 1999. 'Managing Codified'.

26 Abhayawansa, Subhash, and Indra Abeysekera. 2009. 'Intellectual Capital Disclosure from Sell-side Analyst Perspective'. *Journal of Intellectual Capital* 10 (2): 294–306. https://doi.org/10.1108/14691930910952678.

27 Steenkamp, Natasja, and Varsha Kashyap. 2010. 'Importance and Contribution of Intangible Assets: SME Managers' Perceptions'. *Journal of Intellectual Capital* 11 (3): 368–90.

28 Starovic and Marr. 2003. 'Understanding Corporate Value'.

3   Vacancies
1   Australian Bureau of Statistics. 2006. 'Media Release - Boom in Western Australia's Workforce'. 1367.5. Canberra, A.C.T: ABS.
2   Australian Bureau of Statistics. 2007. 'The Resources Industry in Western Australia 2001–02 to 2005–06'. 1367.5. Canberra, A.C.T: ABS.
3   Australian Bureau of Statistics. 2020. 'Job Vacancies, Australia, 2018'. 6354.0. Canberra, A.C.T: ABS.
4   Statistics Canada. 2018. 'Estimates of the Components of International Migration, Quarterly'. Government of Canada. https://www150.statcan.gc.ca/t1/tbl1/en/tv.action?pid=1710004001
5   Office for National Statistics. 2018. 'Migration Statistics Quarterly Report'. Migration Statistics Quarterly Report: July 2018. Office for National Statistics. https://www.ons.gov.uk/peoplepopulationandcommunity/populationandmigration/internationalmigration/bulletins/migrationstatisticsquarterlyreport/july2018revisedfrommaycoveringtheperiodtodecember2017.

4   Globalisation
1   Phillips 2008. 'How the Government'.
2   Department of Mines and Petroleum. 2014. 'Statistics Digest 2014'. Guidance. DMP. http://www.dmp.wa.gov.au/Documents/About-Us-Careers/Statistics_Digest_2014.pdf.
3   Hatch and Cunliffe. 2013. *Organization Theory*, 74.
4   Higgins, Colin, and Philippe Debroux. 2009. 'Globalization and CSR in Asia'. *Asian Business & Management* 8 (2): 125.; Steger, Manfred. 2005. 'Ideologies of Globalization'. *Journal of Political Ideologies* 10 (1): 11.
5   Kalkan 2008. 'An Overall View'.
6   Fahey, Liam, and Laurence Prusak. 1998. 'The Eleven Deadliest Sins of Knowledge Management'. *California Management Review* 40 (4): 265–76.; Herbane, Brahim, Dominic Elliot, and Ethné Swartz. 1996. 'Contingency and Continua: Achieving Excellence Through Business Continuity Planning'. *Businss Horizons* 40 (6): 19–25.; Staber, Udo, and Jörg Sydow. 2002. 'Organizational Adaptive Capacity: A Structuration Perspective'. *Journal of Management Inquiry* 11 (4): 408–24.
7   Canadan International Council. 2014. 'The 9 Habits of Highly Effective Resource Economies: Lessons for Canada'. Canadian International Council. http://opencanada.org/reports/the-9-habits-of-highly-effective-

resource-economies, 67.

8 Slaper, Timothy F, and Tanya J Hall. 2011. 'The Triple Bottom Line: What Is It and How Does It Work'. *Indiana Business Review* 86 (1): 4–8.

9 Kumar, Satish, and Ritesh Tiwari. 2011. 'Corporate Social Responsibility: Insights into Contemporary Research'. *The IUP Journal of Corporate Governance* 10 (1). https://doi.org/04J-2011-01-02-01.

10 Wagner, Tillmann, Richard J. Lutz, and Barton A Weitz. 2009. 'Corporate Hypocrisy: Overcoming the Threat of Inconsistent Corporate Social Responsibility Perceptions'. *Journal of Marketing* 73 (November): 77–91.

11 Carroll, Archie B. 1979. 'A Three-Dimensional Conceptual Model of Corporate Performance'. *Academy of Management Review* 4 (4): 497–505.

12 Coronado, Gabriela, and Wayne Fallon. 2010. 'Giving with One Hand On the Mining Sector's Treatment of Indigenous Stakeholders in the Name of CSR'. *International Journal of Sociology and Social Policy* 30 (11/12): 666–82. https://doi.org/10.1108/01443331011085259.

13 Elkind, Peter, David Whitford, and Doris Burke. 2011. 'BP: "An Accident Waiting to Happen"'. *Fortune*, 24 January 2011.

14 Hoyle, Rhiannon. n.d. 'Financial Impact of Brazil Dam Catastrophe Weighs on BHP Billiton'. *The Australian Business Review*. Accessed 11 October 2015. http://www.theaustralian.com.au/business/mining-energy/financial-impact-of-brazil-dam-disaster-weighs-on-bhp-billiton/story-e6frg9df-1227602579037.

15 D'Aveni 2010. *Hypercompetition*

16 Bartholomeusz, Stephen. 2015. 'A Missed Opportunity for Marginal Iron Ore Producers'. *Business Spectator*, 2015. http://www.businessspectator.com.au/article/2015/6/22/resources-and-energy/missed-opportunity-marginal-iron-ore-producers.; Latimer, Cole. n.d. 'FMG Slam Rio and BHP for "plans" to Flood Iron Ore Market - Australian Mining'. *Australian Mining*. Accessed 21 July 2015. https://www.australianmining.com.au/news/%E2%80%8Bfmg-slam-rio-and-bhp-for-plans-to-flood-iron-ore-market/.

5 Migration

1 Australian Bureau of Statistics. 2020. 'Migration, Australia, 2018-19'. 3412.01. Canberra, A.C.T: ABS.

2 Department of Immigration and Border Protection. 2015. 'Temporary Work (Skilled) Visa (Subclass 457)'. 2015.

https://immi.homeaffairs.gov.au/visas/getting-a-visa/visa-listing/repealed-visas/temporary-work-skilled-457.

3   Bahn, Susanne, Llandis Barratt-Pugh, and Ghialy Yap. 2012. 'The Employment of Skilled Migrants on Temporary 457 Visas in Australia: Emerging Issues'. *Labour & Industry: A Journal of the Social and Economic Relations of Work* 22 (4): 379–398.,3.

4   Canadian International Council 2014. 'The 9 Habits',3.

5   Phillips 2008. 'How the Government',19.

6   Canadian International Council 2014. 'The 9 Habits'.

7   British Geological Survey. 2018. 'World Mineral Statistics | MineralsUK'. World Mineral Production 2012-2016. British Geological Survey. https://www.bgs.ac.uk/mineralsUK/statistics/worldStatistics.html.

8   Australian Bureau of Statistics. 2020. 'Migration, Australia'.

9   Ibid

10 Canadian International Council 2014. 'The 9 Habits'.

11 Ibid, 74.

12 Sirmon, David G, Michael A Hitt, R Duane Ireland, and Brett Anitra Gilbert. 2011. 'Resource Orchestration to Create Competitive Advantage: Breadth, Depth, and Life Cycle Effects'. *Journal of Management* 37 (5): 1390–1412.

13 Pieterse, Jan Nederveen. 2015. *Globalization and Culture: Global Mélange*. Edited by Susan McEachern. 3rd ed. Lanham, Maryland USA: Rowman & Littlefield.

14 Ireland, R Duane, and Michael A Hitt. 1999. 'Achieving and Maintaining Strategic Competitiveness in the 21st Century: The Role of Strategic Leadership'. *Academy of Management Journal* 13 (1): 43–57. ; Sirmon, Hitt, Ireland and Anitra. 2011. 'Resource Orchestration'.

15 Bettis, Richard A, and Michael A Hitt. 1995. 'The New Competitive Landscape'. *Strategic Management Journal* 16: 7–19.

16 Statistics Canada. 2018. 'Estimates of the'.

17 Ibid

18 Office For National Statistics. 2018. 'Migration Statistics Quarterly'.

19 Ibid

6   Complexity Leadership Overview

1   Plowman, Donde Ashmos, and Dennis Duchon. 2007. 'Emergent Leadership: Getting Beyond Heroes and Scapegoats'. In *Complex Systems*

Leadership Theory New Perspectives from Complexity Science on Social and Organizational Effectiveness, edited by James K. Hazy, Jeffrey A. Goldstein, and Benyamin B. Lichtenstein, 1:109–28. ISCE Publishing.
2 Marion, Russ, and Mary Uhl-Bien. 2001. 'Leadership in Complex Organisations'. *The Leadership Quarterly* 12 (4): 389–418.
3 Plowman and Duchon, 2007. 'Emergent Leadership'.
4 Uhl-Bien, Mary, Russ Marion, and Bill McKelvey. 2007. 'Complexity Leadership Theory: Shifting Leadership from the Industrial Age to the Knowledge Era'. *The Leadership Quarterly* 18: 298–318.
5 Plowman and Duchon. 2007. 'Emergent Leadership'.
6 Marr, Bernard, Gianni Schiuma, and Andy Neely. 2004. 'Intellectual Capital - Defining Key Performance Indicators for Organizational Knowledge Assets'. *Business Process Management Journal* 10 (5): 551–69.
7 Solesvik, Marina. 2015. 'Paradigm Change in Strategic Management Research: Is the Resource-Based View a New Theory of Firm?' *Available at SSRN 2631769*, August. http://www.researchgate.net.
8 Lim, David, and Jane Klobas. 2000. 'Knowledge Management in Small Enterprises'. *The Electronic Library*.

7 Corporate Social Responsibility
1 Kumar and Tiwari. 2011. 'Corporate Social'.
2 Wagner, Lutz and Weitz. 2009. 'Corporate Hypocrisy'.
3 Frazier, Mya. 2008. 'Who's in Charge of Green'. *Advertising Age* 79 (23): S1–2.
4 Foote, Jessica, Nolan Gaffney, and James R. Evans. 2010. 'Corporate Social Responsibility: Implications for Performance Excellence'. *Total Quality Management* 21 (8): 799–812.
5 Matten, Dirk, and Jeremy Moon. 2008. '"Implicit" and "Explicit" CSR: A Conceptual Framework for A Comparative Understanding of Corporate Social Responsibility'. *Academy of Management Review* 33 (2): 404–24.
6 Ibid
7 Escobar, Luis Fernando, and Harrie Vredenburg. 2010. 'Multinational Oil Companies and the Adoption of Sustainable Development: A Resource-Based and Institutional Theory Interpretation of Adoption Heterogeneity'. *Journal of Business Ethics* 98: 39–65.; Hatch and Cunliffe. 2013. *Organization Theory.*

8   Foote, Gaffney, and Evans. 2010. 'Corporate Social Responsibility'.
9   Hatch and Cunliffe. 2013. *Organization Theory,* 216.
10   Ehrgott, Matthias, Felix Reimann, Lutz Kaufmann, and Craig R. Carter.
     2011. 'Social Sustainability in Selecting Emerging Economy Suppliers'.
     Journal of Business Ethics 98: 99–119.
11   Wheeler, David, and Maria Sillanpää. 1997. *The Stakeholder Corporation:
     A Blueprint for Maximizing Stakeholder Value*. Pitman.
12   Tamm, Katrin, Raul Eamets, and Pille Mõtsmees. 2010. 'Relationship
     between Corporate Social Responsibility and Job Satisfaction: The Case of
     Baltic Countries'. *The University of Tartu Faculty of Economics and
     Business Administration Working Paper*, no. 76–2010.
13   Escobar and Vredenburg. 2010. 'Multinational Oil Companies'.
14   Starovic and Marr. 2003. 'Understanding Corporate Value'.
15   Canadian International Council 2014. 'The 9 Habits'.

8   Summary

1   Australian Bureau of Statistics. 2002. 'The Resources Industry'.

Part Two: The Resources Sector

9   Western Australia

1   Smith, David A. 2005. 'Starting at the Beginning: Extractive Economies as
     the Unexamined Origins of Global Commodity Chains'. In *Global Shift:
     Mapping the Changing Contours of the World Economy*, edited by Peter
     Dicken, 10:243–66. SAGE Publications Ltd.
2   Australian Bureau of Statistics. 2002. 'The Resources Industry'.
3   Department of Mines and Petroleum. 2014. 'Statistics Digest 2014', 2.
4   Australian Bureau of Statistics. 2007. 'The Resources Industry'.
5   Department of Mines and Petroleum. 2014. 'Statistics Digest 2014'
6   Department of Mines and Petroleum. 2019. 'Statistics Digest 2018-19'.
     Guidance. DMP. http://www.dmp.wa.gov.au/Documents/About-Us-
     Careers/Statistics_Digest_2018-19.pdf.
7   Canadian International Council 2014. 'The 9 Habits'.
8   Sharpe, Andrew, and Blair Long. 2012. 'Innovation in Canadian Natural
     Resource Industries: A Systems-Based Analysis of Performance, Policy
     and Emerging Challenges'. Centre for the Study of Living Standards.
     http://www.csls.ca.
9   Department of Mines and Petroleum. 2014. 'Statistics Digest 2014', 2.

10 'Mid-Tier Miners under Pressure'. 2008. SmartCompany. 17 June 2008. https://www.smartcompany.com.au/finance/economy/mid-tier-miners-under-pressure/.
11 'Time Series Financial Search. DatAnalysisPremium'. 2016. http://datanalysis.morningstar.com.au.

10 The Study Context
1   Smith 2005. 'Starting at the Beginning'.
2   Ashmos, Donde P., Dennis Duchon, Reuben R. McDaniel Jr., and John W. Huonker. 2002. 'What a Mess! Participation as a Simple Managerial Rule to "Complexify" Organizations'. *Journal of Management Studies* 39 (2): 189–206. https://doi.org/10.1111/1467-6486.00288, 192.
3   Granovetter, Mark S. 1973. 'The Strength of Weak Ties'. *American Journal of Sociology* 78 (6): 1360–80. http://sociology.stanford.edu, 1361.
4   Panzar, Carmen, James K. Hazy, Bill McKelvey, and David R. Schwandt. 2007. 'The Paradox of Complex Organizations: Leadership as Integrative Influence'. In *Complex Systems Leadership Theory New Perspectives from Complexity Science on Social and Organizational Effectiveness*, edited by James K. Hazy, Jeffrey A. Goldstein, and Benyamin B. Lichtenstein, 1:305–26. ISCE Publishing.
5   Kalkan 2008. 'An Overall View'.
6   Nonaka, Ikujiro. 1991. 'The Knowledge-Creating Company'. *Harvard Business Review* 69 (6): 96.
7   Ibid

11 Innovation in the Resources Sector
1   Kumar and Tiwari. 2011. 'Corporate Social'
2   Escobar and Vredenburg. 2010. 'Multinational Oil Companies'.
3   Sharpe and Long. 2012. 'Innovation in Canadian', 9.
4   Ibid
5   Ibid
6   Fischer, Manfred M., and Josef Fröhlich, eds. 2013. *Knowledge, Complexity and Innovation Systems*. Springer Science & Business Media.
7   Levitt, Theodore. 1965. 'Exploit the Product Life Cycle'. *Harvard Business Review*, 1 November 1965. https://hbr.org/1965/11/exploit-the-product-life-cycle.; Gaubinger, Kurt, Michael Rabl, Scott Swan, and Thomas Werani. 2015. 'Life Cycle Management'. In *Innovation and*

Product Management, 207–220. Springer, 208.

8   Environment and Climate Change Canada. 2009. 'Environmental Code of Practice for Metal Mines'. Guidance. http://www.publications.gc.ca/site/eng/9.691856/publication.html.

9   Canadian International Council 2014. 'The 9 Habits'.

10 Australian Bureau of Statistics. 2002. 'The Resources Industry'.

11 Kianto, Aino, Pia Hurmelinna-Laukkanen, and Paavo Ritala. 2010. 'Intellectual Capital in Service- and Product-oriented Companies'. *Journal of Intellectual Capital* 11 (3): 305–25. https://doi.org/10.1108/14691931011064563, 316.

12 Kogut, Bruce. 1985. 'Designing Global Strategies: Comparative and Competitive Value-Added Chains'. *Sloan Management Review (Pre-1986)* 26 (4): 15.; Lin, Yen-Ting, Ali K Parlaktürk, and Jayashankar M Swaminathan. 2014. 'Vertical Integration under Competition: Forward, Backward, or No Integration?' *Production and Operations Management* 23 (1): 19–35.

13 Sharpe and Long. 2012. 'Innovation in Canadian'.

Part Three: Cybernetic Leadership

1   Liang, Thow Yick. 2015. 'Relativistic Complexity, Adaptive Governance and the Intelligence Leadership'. *Human Systems Management* 34 (3): 201–223, 202.

2   Plowman, and Duchon. 2007. 'Emergent Leadership'.

3   Uhl-Bien, Marion and McKelvey. 2007. 'Complexity Leadership Theory'.

4   Dwyer, Patrick C, Joyce E Bono, Mark Snyder, Oded Nov, and Yair Berson. 2013. 'Sources of Volunteer Motivation: Transformational Leadership and Personal Motives Influence Volunteer Outcomes'. *Nonprofit Management and Leadership* 24 (2): 181–205.; Yukl, Gary. 1999. 'An Evaluation of Conceptual Weaknesses in Transformational and Charismatic Leadership Theories'. *The Leadership Quarterly* 10 (2): 285–305.

5   Uhl-Bien, Marion and McKelvey. 2007. 'Complexity Leadership Theory'

6   Bass, Bernard M. 1990. 'From Transactional to Transformational Leadership: Learning to Share the Vision'. *Organizational Dynamics* 18 (3): 19–31.; Kanungo, Rabindra N. 2001. 'Ethical Values of Transactional and Transformational Leaders'. *Canadian Journal of Administrative*

Sciences 18 (4): 257.
7 Ibid
8 Allen, Thomas J, Peter Gloor, Andrea Fronzetti Colladon, Stephanie L Woerner, and Ornit Raz. 2016. 'The Power of Reciprocal Knowledge Sharing Relationships for Startup Success'. *Journal of Small Business and Enterprise Development* 23 (3): 636–51.; Ibid
9 Waddell, Alex, and Edwina Pio. 2015. 'The Influence of Senior Leaders on Organisational Learning: Insights from the Employees' Perspective'. *Management Learning* 46 (4): 461–478.
10 Allio, Robert J. 2008. 'A Conversation with Gary Hamel'. *Strategy & Leadership* 36 (2): 5–10.
11 Ibid
12 Meindl, James R, Sanford B Ehrlich, and Janet M Dukerich. 1985. 'The Romance of Leadership'. *Administrative Science Quarterly* 30: 78–102.; Nan, Ning, Robert Zmud, and Emre Yetgin. 2014. 'A Complex Adaptive Systems Perspective of Innovation Diffusion: An Integrated Theory and Validated Virtual Laboratory'. *Computational and Mathematical Organization Theory* 20 (1): 52–88.

13 Distribution

1 Knoke, Benjamin, Thorsten Wuest, and Klaus-Dieter Thoben. 2013. 'Fragmented Knowledge in Collaborative Manufacturing Process Chains'. In *2013 International Conference on Collaboration Technologies and Systems (CTS)*, 451–456. IEEE. ; Zack 1999. 'Managing Codified Knowledge'.
2 Bettiol, Marco, Eleonora Di Maria, and Roberto Grandinetti. 2012. 'Codification and Creativity: Knowledge Management Strategies in KIBS'. *Journal of Knowledge Management* 16 (4): 550–562.
3 Surie, Gita, and James K. Hazy. 2006. 'Generative Leadership: Nurturing Innovation in Complex Systems'. *E:CO* 8 (4): 13–26.
4 Mueller, Andreas, and Michael Schade. 2012. 'Symbols and Place Identity: A Semiotic Approach to Internal Place Branding-Case Study Bremen (Germany)'. *Journal of Place Management and Development* 5 (1): 81–92.
.

14 Functional Participation

1 Andrews, Gwen, and Richard N Knowles. 2011. 'A Practical East-West Exploration Of Leadership And Learning.' *E:CO* 13 (4): 1–17.

2   Nonaka 1991. 'The Knowledge-Creating'.
3   Uhl-Bien, Marion and McKelvey. 2007. 'Complexity Leadership Theory'.
4   Ibid
5   Andrews and Knowles. 2011. 'Practical East-West'.
6   Davenport, Thomas H. 1993. 'Process Innovation: Reengineering Work through Information Technology'. *Harvard Business School Press, Boston.* ;Staw, Barry M. 1980. 'The Consequences of Turnover'. *Journal of Occupational Behaviour* 1 (4): 253–273. http://www.jstor.org/stable/3000143.
7   Bolino, Turnley and Bloodgood. 2002. 'Citizenship Behaviour'.

15 Enabling Leadership

1   Lloyd, Bruce, and Thomas A Stewart. 2002. 'Leadership and Knowledge Management'. *Leadership & Organization Development Journal* 23 (5): 288.
2   Uhl-Bien, Marion and McKelvey 2007. 'Complexity Leadership Theory'.
3   Schreiber, Craig, and Kathleen M. Carley. 2006. 'Leadership Style as an Enabler of Organizational Complex Functioning'. *E:CO* 8 (4): 61–76.

16 Workers

1   Drucker, Peter F. 1992. 'The New Society of Organizations.' *Harvard Business Review* 70 (5): 95. , 100; Drucker, Peter F. 1998. 'Management's New Paradigms'. *Forbes Magazine* 10 (2): 98–99.
2   Drucker 1999. 'Knowledge-Worker Productivity'.
3   Roper, Kathy. 2013. 'Educational Implications of an FM Social Constructionist View'. In *Managing Organizational Ecologies: Space, Management, and Organizations*, edited by Keith Alexander and Ilfryn Price, 207–216. Routledge. ; Ulrich, Dave. 1998. 'Intellectual Capital= Competence x Commitment'. *MIT Sloan Management Review* 39 (2): 15.
4   Nonaka 1991. 'The Knowledge-Creating'.
5   Ashmos, Donde P., Dennis Duchon, Reuben R. McDaniel Jr., and John W. Huonker. 2002. 'What a Mess! Participation as a Simple Managerial Rule to "Complexify" Organizations'. *Journal of Management Studies* 39 (2): 189–206. https://doi.org/10.1111/1467-6486.00288, 192.
6   Hatch and Cunliffe 2013. *Organization Theory*, 76.

17 Consult and Engage
1 Heifetz, Ronald, Alexander Grashow, and Marty Linsky. 2009. *The Practice of Adaptive Leadership*. Boston, MA: Cambridge Leadership Associates,153.
2 Morrison, Elizabeth W. 2011. 'Employee Voice Behavior: Integration and Directions for Future Research'. *Academy of Management Annals* 5 (1): 373–412.
3 Ulrich 1998. 'Intellectual Capital'.
4 Nahapiet, Janine, and Sumantra Ghoshal. 1998. 'Social Capital, Intellectual Capital, and the Organizational Advantage'. *Academy of Management Review* 23 (2): 242–67.
5 Allen, Peter. 2001. 'What Is Complexity Science? Knowledge of the Limits to Knowledge'. *Emergence, A Journal of Complexity Issues in Organizations and Management* 3 (1): 24–42.
6 Lord, Robert G. 2008. 'Beyond Transactional and Transformational Leadership: Can Leaders Still Lead When They Don't Know What to Do'. In *Complexity Leadership Part 1: Conceptual Foundations*, edited by Mary Uhl-Bien and Russ Marion, 155–84. IAP - Information Age Publishing, Inc.
7 Eiser, J Richard. 1994. 'Attitudes, Chaos and the Connectionist Mind.' In *Complexity Leadership Part I: Conceptual Foundations*, edited by Mary Uhl-Bien and Russ Marion. Charlotte, NC: IAP - Information Age Publishing, Inc.; Summers, James K, Stephen E Humphrey, and Gerald R Ferris. 2012. 'Team Member Change, Flux in Coordination, and Performance: Effects of Strategic Core Roles, Information Transfer, and Cognitive Ability'. *Academy of Management Journal* 55 (2): 314–338.

18 Taken for Granted
1 Taylor, Frederick Winslow. 2012. *Principles of Scientific Management*. Auckland, NZ: The Floating Press., 74.
2 Robinson, Sandra L., and Denise M. Rousseau. 1994. 'Violating the Psychological Contract :Not the Exception but the Norm'. *Journal of Organizational Behavior* 15: 245–49.; Rousseau, Denise M. 1989. 'Psychological and Implied Contracts in Organizations'. *Employee Responsibilities and Rights Journal* 2 (2): 121–139.,128.
3 Education and Health Standing Committee. 2015. 'The Impact of FIFO Work Practices on Mental Health: Final Report'. Parliament of Western

Australia. www.parliament.wa.gov.au.,94.

4   Wiley, Carolyn. 1997. 'What Motivates Employees According to over 40 Years of Motivation Surveys'. *International Journal of Manpower* 18 (3): 263–80.

5   Bhatnagar, Jyotsna. 2012. 'Management of Innovation: Role of Psychological Empowerment, Work Engagement and Turnover Intention in the Indian Context'. *The International Journal of Human Resource Management* 23 (5): 928–951., 929.

6   Conger, Jay A, and Rabindra N Kanungo. 1988. 'The Empowerment Process: Integrating Theory and Practice'. *Academy of Management Review* 13 (3): 471–482., 474.

7   Bhatnagar 2012. 'Management of Innovation', 929.

8   Morrison 2011. 'Employee Voice Behavior', 405.

19   Empowerment

1   Gurteen, David. 1998. 'Knowledge, Creativity and Innovation'. *Journal of Knowledge Management* 2 (1): 5–13.; West, Michael A, and Claudia A Sacramento. 2012. 'Creativity and Innovation: The Role of Team and Organizational Climate', 359–385. https://research.aston.ac.uk/portal/en/researchoutput/creativity-and-innovation.html.

20   Respect

1   Plowman and Duchon 2007. 'Emergent Leadership'.

2   Gurteen 1998. 'Knowledge'; Shalley, Christina E, Lucy L Gilson, and Terry C Blum. 2009. 'Interactive Effects of Growth Need Strength, Work Context, and Job Complexity on Self-Reported Creative Performance'. *Academy of Management Journal* 52 (3): 489–505.

3   Gurteen 1998. 'Knowledge'; Tierney, William G, and Michael Lanford. 2015. 'Creativity and Innovation in the Twenty-Firstcentury University'. In *Researching Higher Education: International Perspectives on Theory, Policy and Practice*, edited by Jennifer M. Case and Jeroen Huisman, 61. Oxon, UK: Routledge.

4   Amabile, Teresa M. 1983. 'The Social Psychology of Creativity: A Componential Conceptualization.' *Journal of Personality and Social Psychology* 45 (2): 357–76., 360.

5   Stein, Morris I. 1953. 'Creativity and Culture'. *The Journal of Psychology*

36 (2): 311–322., 311.
6   Audretsch, David B, Clara Martínez-Fuentes, and Manuela Pardo-del-Val. 2011. 'Incremental Innovation in Services through Continuous Improvement'. *The Service Industries Journal* 31 (12): 1921–1930.
7   Ibid, 1922.
8   Jiménez-Jiménez, Daniel, and Raquel Sanz-Valle. 2011. 'Innovation, Organizational Learning, and Performance'. *Journal of Business Research* 64 (4): 408–417.
9   Caetano, Ana. 2019. 'Designing Social Action: The Impact of Reflexivity on Practice'. *Journal for the Theory of Social Behaviour* 49 (2): 146–160. https://doi.org/doi:10.1111/jtsb.12196.
10 Jiménez-Jiménez, Daniel, and Raquel Sanz-Valle. 2011. 'Innovation, organizational learning, and performance.'
11 Stein 1953. 'Creativity', 312.
12 Caroline Martins, Ellen, and Hester WJ Meyer. 2012. 'Organizational and Behavioral Factors That Influence Knowledge Retention'. *Journal of Knowledge Management* 16 (1): 77–96.; Shalley, Gilson, and Blum. 2009. 'Interactive Effects'; Ulrich, Dave. 1998. 'Intellectual Capital'.

21 Right People
1   Gebauer, Heiko, Hagen Worch, and Bernhard Truffer. 2014. 'Value Innovations in Electricity Utilities'. In *Framing Innovation in Public Service Sectors*, edited by Rolf Rønning, Bo Enquist, and Lars Fuglsang, 85–111. New York, NY: Routledge.; Ulrich, Dave. 1998. 'Intellectual Capital'.
2   Dess, Gregory G, and Jason D Shaw. 2001. 'Voluntary Turnover, Social Capital, and Organizational Performance'. *Academy of Management Review* 26 (3): 446–456.
3   Pfeffer and Sutton 2013. *The knowing-doing gap.*
4   Kavanagh, Carol. 2014. 'Culture of Collaboration Improves Safety and Efficiency at Travis Perkins: Company-Wide Engagement Proves a Winner for Business, Colleagues and Customers'. *Human Resource Management International Digest* 22 (4): 8–11.
5   De Beer, Frank, and Daniel Hercules Du Toit. 2015. 'Human Resources Managers as Custodians of the King III Code'. *South African Journal of Economic and Management Sciences* 18 (2): 206–217., 210.
6   McCauley, Cindy, and Michael Wakefield. 2006. 'Talent Management in

the 21st Century: Help Your Company Find, Develop, and Keep Its Strongest Workers'. *The Journal for Quality and Participation* 29 (4): 4–7.

7   Hessen, Corey N, and Brian J Lewis. 2001. 'Steps You Can Take to Hire, Keep, and Inspire Generation Xers'. *Leadership and Management in Engineering* 1 (1): 42–44.

8   Ribiere, Vincent M, and Aleša Saša Sitar. 2004. 'Critical Role of Leadership in Nurturing a Knowledge-Supporting Culture'. *Knowledge Management Research and Practice* 1 (1): 39.

9   Kalkan 2008. 'An Overall View'.

10 DePree, Max. 2003. *Leading without Power: Finding Hope in Serving Community*. 2nd ed. Michigan, US: Jossey-Bass.

11 Caroline Martins and Meyer 2012. 'Organizational and behavioural'; Ulrich 1998. 'Intellectual Capital'.

12 Casimir, Gian, Karen Lee, and Mark Loon. 2012. 'Knowledge Sharing: Influences of Trust, Commitment and Cost'. *Journal of Knowledge Management* 16 (5): 740–53.; Gurteen 1998. 'Knowledge'.

13 Patulny, Roger. 2011. 'Social Trust, Social Partner Time and Television Time'. *Social Indicators Research* 101 (2): 289–293.

22 Team

1   Marion and Uhl-Bien. 2001. 'Leadership in Complex Organisations'.

2   Cooke, Nancy J, Preston A Kiekel, and Erin E Helm. 2001. 'Measuring Team Knowledge during Skill Acquisition of a Complex Task'. *International Journal of Cognitive Ergonomics* 5 (3): 297–315.; Staw 1980. 'The Consequences of Turnover'.

3   Henao, César Augusto, Juan Carlos Muñoz, and Juan Carlos Ferrer. 2015. 'The Impact of Multi-Skilling on Personnel Scheduling in the Service Sector: A Retail Industry Case'. *Journal of the Operational Research Society* 66 (12): 1949–1959. https://doi.org/doi:10.1057/jors.2015.9.; Staw 1980. 'The Consequences of Turnover'.

4   Jones, Rhonda. 2010. 'Social Capital: Bridging the Link between Talent Management and Knowledge Management'. In *Smart Talent Management: Building Knowledge Assets for Competitive Advantage*, edited by Vlad Vaiman and Charles M Vance, 217–33. Edward Elgar Publishing , 210.

5   Nishiguchi, Toshihiro, and Ikujirō Nonaka. 2000. *Knowledge Emergence: Social, Technical, and Evolutionary Dimensions of Knowledge Creation*. New York, NY: Oxford University Press., 5.

6   Ibid
7   Ibid,38.
8   Brunold, Julia, and Susanne Durst. 2012. 'Intellectual Capital Risks and Job Rotation'. *Journal of Intellectual Capital* 13 (2): 178–95.
9   Ibid
10 Ibid

23 Tenure
1   Pfeffer, Jeffrey. 1985. 'Organizational Demography: Implications for Management'. *California Management Review* 28 (1): 67–81.
2   Staw 1980. 'The Consequences of Turnover'.
3   Ibid
4   Grote, Richard C. 2005. *Forced Ranking: Making Performance Management Work*. Harvard Business School Press Boston, MA.

24 Operationalising
1   Caroline Martins and Meyer 2012. 'Organizational and behavioural'; Ulrich 1998. 'Intellectual Capital'.
2   Nonaka 1991. 'The Knowledge-Creating Company', 96.
3   Ibid
4   Kang, Sung-Choon, and Scott A Snell. 2009. 'Intellectual Capital Architectures and Ambidextrous Learning: A Framework for Human Resource Management'. *Journal of Management Studies* 46 (1): 65–92., 68.
5   Caroline Martins and Meyer 2012. 'Organizational and behavioural'
6   Brown, John Seely, and Paul Duguid. 1991. 'Organizational Learning and Communities-of-Practice: Toward a Unified View of Working, Learning, and Innovation'. *Organization Science* 2 (1): 40–57.; Feldman, Martha S, and James G March. 1981. 'Information in Organizations as Signal and Symbol'. *Administrative Science Quarterly* 26: 171–186. http://uci.edu.; Rangan, Subramanian, ed. 2015. *Performance and Progress: Essays on Capitalism, Business, and Society*. OUP Oxford.
7   Adler, Paul S. 1989. 'When Knowledge Is the Critical Resource, Knowledge Management Is the Critical Task'. *IEEE Transactions on Engineering Management* 36 (2): 87–94., 93.
8   Frankel, Jeffrey A. 2012. 'The Natural Resource Curse: A Survey of Diagnoses and Some Prescriptions'. *HKS Faculty Research Working Paper*

Series. https://dash.harvard.edu/handle/1/8694932., 2.

9   Sheerin, Kirsty. 2014. 'Employment Longevity in the Mining Industry-a
Perspective for New Mining Graduates'. *AusIMM Bulletin*, no. 6: 40.
http://www.srk.co.id.

10   Ulrich 1998. 'Intellectual Capital'; Schmitt, Achim, Stefano Borzillo, and
Gilbert Probst. 2012. 'Don't Let Knowledge Walk Away: Knowledge
Retention during Employee Downsizing'. *Management Learning* 43 (1):
53–74.

11   Pfeffer 1985. 'Organizational Demography'.

12   Parton, John, and Tim Ryley. 2012. 'A Business Analysis of XL Airways:
What Lessons Can Be Learned from the Failure?' *Journal of Air Transport
Management* 19: 42–48.; Randolph-Seng, Brandon, Ronald K Mitchell,
Alejandra Marin, and Jaehwan H Lee. 2015. 'Job Security and
Entrepreneurship: Enemies or Allies?' *Journal of Applied Management
and Entrepreneurship* 20 (1): 24–49.

13   Nonaka 1991. 'The Knowledge-Creating Company'.

14   Uhl-Bien, Mary, and Russ Marion. 2009. 'Complexity Leadership in
Bureaucratic Forms of Organizing: A Meso Model'. *The Leadership
Quarterley* 20 (4): 631–50.

15   Ibid

16   Cilliers, Paul. 2000. 'Rules and Complex Systems'. *Emergence, A Journal
of Complexity Issues in Organizations and Management* 2 (3): 40–50.

17   Nonaka 1991. 'The Knowledge-Creating Company'.

18   Schreiber and Carley. 2006. 'Leadership Style'.

19   Bezooijen, Bart Van, and Eric-Hans Kramer. 2015. 'Mission Command in
the Information Age: A Normal Accidents Perspective on Networked
Military Operations'. *Journal of Strategic Studies* 38 (4): 445–466.

20   Vogelaar, Ad LW, and Eric-Hans Kramer. 2004. 'Mission Command in
Dutch Peace Support Missions'. *Armed Forces & Society* 30 (3): 409–431.

21   Borzillo, Stefano, and Renata Kaminska-Labbé. 2011. 'Unravelling the
Dynamics of Knowledge Creation in Communities of Practice Though
Complexity Theory Lenses'. *Knowledge Management Research &
Practice* 9 (4): 353–366.

22   Kohn, Nicholas W, and Steven M Smith. 2011. 'Collaborative Fixation:
Effects of Others' Ideas on Brainstorming'. *Applied Cognitive Psychology*
25 (3): 359–371.; Sutton, Robert I, and Andrew Hargadon. 1996.
'Brainstorming Groups in Context: Effectiveness in a Product Design

Firm'. *Administrative Science Quarterly* 41 (4): 685–718.
23 Dennis, Alan R, Randall K Minas, and Akshay P Bhagwatwar. 2013. 'Sparking Creativity: Improving Electronic Brainstorming with Individual Cognitive Priming'. *Journal of Management Information Systems* 29 (4): 195–216., 195.
24 Chesbrough, Henry William. 2006. *Open Innovation: The New Imperative for Creating and Profiting from Technology*. Harvard Business Press., xxiv
25 Ibid
26 Lichtenthaler, Ulrich. 2011. 'Open Innovation: Past Research, Current Debates, and Future Directions'. *Academy of Management Perspectives* 25 (1): 75–93., 82.
27 Levy, Moria. 2011. 'Knowledge Retention: Minimizing Organizational Business Loss'. *Journal of Knowledge Management* 15 (4): 582–600.

25 Encouragement

1 Csath, Magdolna. 2012. 'Encouraging Innovation in Small and Medium Sized Businesses: Learning Matters'. *Development and Learning in Organizations: An International Journal* 26 (5): 9–13.
2 Bolino, Turnley and Bloodgood. 2002. 'Citizenship Behaviour'.
3 Teerikangas, Satu, and Liisa Välikangas. 2013. 'Engaged Employees! An Actor Perspective on Innovation'. In *Handbook of Organizational and Managerial Innovation*, edited by Tyrone S. Pitsis, Ace Simpson, and Erlend Dehlin, 54–97. Edward Elgar Publishing.,80.
4 Ibid., 87.

26 Fear

1 Shinnar, Rachel S, Olivier Giacomin, and Frank Janssen. 2012. 'Entrepreneurial Perceptions and Intentions: The Role of Gender and Culture'. *Entrepreneurship Theory and Practice* 36 (3): 465–493.; Gurteen 1998. 'Knowledge'.
2 McGrath, Jerrold. 2014. 'Four Fears That Stifle Innovation'. 2014. https://medium.com/@jerroldmcgrath/four-fears-that-stifle-innovation-68ccc1d77ac8.
3 Hatch and Cunliffe 2013. *Organization Theory.*
4 Wang, Yijing, and Daniel Laufer. 2020. 'How Does Crisis Management in China Differ from the West?: A Review of the Literature and Directions for Future Research'. *Journal of International Management* 26 (1):

100708.

5   Jonasson, Charlotte, and Jakob Lauring. 2012. 'Cultural Differences in Use: The Power to Essentialize Communication Styles'. *Journal of Communication Management* 16 (4): 405–19. https://doi.org/10.1108/13632541211279030.

6   Ireland and Hitt. 1998. 'Achieving and Maintaining', 53.

27 Openness

1   Lamers, Josee. 2013. 'Work Organisation and Innovation-Case Study: Rabobank, Netherlands'. http://digitalcommons.ilr.cornell.edu/cgi/viewcontent.cgi?article=1256&context=intl.

2   Ulrich 1998. 'Intellectual Capital'; Lin, Carol Yeh-Yun, and Feng-Chuan Liu. 2012. 'A Cross-Level Analysis of Organizational Creativity Climate and Perceived Innovation'. *European Journal of Innovation Management* 15 (1): 55–76.

3   Detert, James R, and Amy C Edmondson. 2011. 'Implicit Voice Theories: Taken-for-Granted Rules of Self-Censorship at Work'. *Academy of Management Journal* 54 (3): 461–488.

4   Ibid

5   Morrison 2011. 'Employee Voice Behavior'.

28 Process

1   Leydesdorff, Loet. 2002. 'The Communication Turn in the Theory of Social Systems'. *Systems Research and Behavioral Science* 19 (2): 129–36. https://doi.org/10.1002/sres.453.; Nonaka, Ikujiro. 1994. 'A Dynamic Theory of Organizational Knowledge Creation'. *Organization Science* 5 (1): 14–37.

2   Starovic, and Marr. 2003. 'Understanding Corporate Value'.

3   Ibid

4   Kalling, Thomas. 2003. 'Organization-Internal Transfer of Knowledge and the Role of Motivation: A Qualitative Case Study'. *Knowledge and Process Management* 10 (2): 115–26. https://doi.org/10.1002/kpm.170.

5   De Long, David W, and Liam Fahey. 2000. 'Diagnosing Cultural Barriers to Knowledge Management'. *Academy of Management Perspectives* 14 (4): 113–127.

29 Structure
1   Weiblen, Tobias, and Henry W Chesbrough. 2015. 'Engaging with Startups to Enhance Corporate Innovation'. *California Management Review* 57 (2): 66–90.

Part Four: Intellectual Capital

30 Individual Characteristics
1   Heifetz, Grashow and Linsky. 2009. *The Practice of Adaptive Leadership* Raney, Ann Fisher. 2014. 'Agility in Adversity: Integrating Mindfulness and Principles of Adaptive Leadership in the Administration of a Community Mental Health Center.' *Clinical Social Work Journal* 42 (3): 312–20.

2   Bornay-Barrachina, Mar, Alvaro López-Cabrales, and Ramón Valle-Cabrera. 2017. 'How Do Employment Relationships Enhance Firm Innovation? The Role of Human and Social Capital'. *The International Journal of Human Resource Management* 28 (9): 1363–1391.;Nahapiet and Ghoshal. 1998. 'Social Capital'.

3   Bornay-Barrachina, López-Cabrales, and Valle-Cabrera. 2017. 'How do employment relationships'.

4   Santagostino, Angelo. 2014. 'The Relations of Human Capital to Economic Growth: A Market Based Approach'. *Journal of European Studies* 30 (1).; Starovic, and Marr. 2003. 'Understanding Corporate Value'.

5   Martín-de-Castro, Gregorio, Miriam Delgado-Verde, Pedro López-Sáez, and José E Navas-López. 2011. 'Towards "an Intellectual Capital-Based View of the Firm": Origins and Nature'. *Journal of Business Ethics* 98 (4): 649–662. .

6   Ibid

7   Hsu, Ya-Hui, and Wenchang Fang. 2009. 'Intellectual Capital and New Product Development Performance: The Mediating Role of Organizational Learning Capability'. *Technological Forecasting and Social Change* 76 (5): 664–677., 665.

8   Ibid; Starovic, and Marr. 2003. 'Understanding Corporate Value', 6.

9   Cabrita, Maria do Rosario, and Nick Bontis. 2008. 'Intellectual Capital and Business Performance in the Portuguese Banking Industry'. *International Journal of Technology Management* 43 (1–3): 212–237. ; Marr, Schiuma, and Neely. 2004. 'Intellectual capital - defining key performance indicators'.

10 Starovic, and Marr. 2003. 'Understanding Corporate Value'.

11 Steenkamp and Kashyap. 2010. 'Importance and contribution'.

12 Ibid

13 Hall, Richard. 1992. 'The Strategic Analysis of Intangible Resources'. *Strategic Management Journal* 13: 135–44.; Maguire, Jackie. 2008. 'Intellectual Capital: Not a Black and White Issue-[Management Inventions]'. *Engineering & Technology* 3 (19): 76–77.

14 Zohar, Danah. 1997. *Rewiring the Corporate Brain: Using the New Science to Rethink How We Structure and Lead Organizations.* Berrett-Koehler Publishers., 10.

15 Ibid, 18.

16 Hsu and Fang. 2009, 'Intellectual Capital'; Nahapiet and Ghoshal. 1998. 'Social Capital'.

17 Starovic, and Marr. 2003. 'Understanding Corporate Value'.

18 Baker, Ellen, Jenny Onyx, and Melissa Edwards. 2011. 'Emergence, Social Capital And Entrepreneurship: Understanding Networks From The Inside'. *E:CO* 13 (3): 21–38.; Nahapiet and Ghoshal. 1998. 'Social Capital'.

19 Deng, Wendong, and George Hendrikse. 2014. 'Cooperative Social Capital-towards a Lifecycle Perspective'. In . European Association of Agricultural Economists.

20 Smith, Carol, Marie de Beer, and Roger Bruce Mason. 2015. 'Tacit Knowledge Sharing Behavior, within a Relational Social Capital Framework, in a South African University of Technology'. *Journal of Applied Business Research (JABR)* 31 (6): 2091–2106.

21 Hitt, Michael A, Barbara W Keats, and Samuel M DeMarie. 1998. 'Navigating in the New Competitive Landscape: Building Strategic Flexibility and Competitive Advantage in the 21st Century'. *The Academy of Management Perspectives* 12 (4): 22–42.

22 Chambers, Elizabeth G, Mark Foulon, Helen Handfield-Jones, Steven M Hankin, and Edward G Michaels. 1998. 'The War for Talent'. *McKinsey Quarterly* 3: 44–57.

23 Allio 2008. 'A Conversation with Gary Hamel.'

24 Molloy, Janice C, and Jay Bryan Barney. 2015. 'Who Captures the Value Created with Human Capital? A Market-Based View'. *Academy of Management Perspectives* 29 (3): 309–325.

25 Oldroyd, James B, and Shad S Morris. 2012. 'Catching Falling Stars: A Human Resource Response to Social Capital's Detrimental Effect of Information Overload on Star Employees'. *Academy of Management*

Review 37 (3): 396–418.
26 Dess and Shaw. 2001. 'Voluntary Turnover, Social Capital'; Ton, Zeynep, and Robert S Huckman. 2008. 'Managing the Impact of Employee Turnover on Performance; The Role of Process Conformance'. *Organisation Science* 19 (1): 56–58.
27 Dess and Shaw. 2001. 'Voluntary Turnover, Social Capital'; Massingham 2008. 'Measuring the Impact'.
28 Schreiber and Carley. 2006. 'Leadership Style'.

Part Five: Structural Capital

32 Resources
1 Boschetti, Fabio, Pierre-Yves Hardy, Nicola Grigg, and Pierre Horwitz. 2011. 'Can We Learn How Complex Systems Work?' *E:CO* 13 (4): 47–62.
2 Gonnering, Russell S. 2010. 'The Seductive Allure of "Best Practices": Improved Outcome Is a Delicate Dance between Structure and Process'. *E:CO* 13 (4): 94–101.
3 Nahapiet and Ghoshal. 1998. 'Social Capital'.
4 Jonasson and Lauring. 2012. 'Cultural Differences', 413.
5 Boal, Kimberly B., and Patrick L. Schultz. 2007. 'Storytelling, Time, and Evolution: The Role of Strategic Leadership in Complex Adaptive Systems'. *The Leadership Quarterly* 18: 411–28.

33 Utilising
1 Hunt, James G. (Jerry), Richard N Osborn, and Kimberly B Boal. 2009. 'The Architecture of Managerial Leadership: Stimulation and Channeling of Organisational Emergence'. *The Leadership Quarterly* 20: 503–16. https://doi.org/10.1016/j.leaqua.2009.04.2010.
2 Leana, Carrie R, and Harry J Van Buren III. 1999. 'Organisational Social Capital and Employment Practices'. *Academy of Management Review* 24 (3): 538–55.
3 MacGillivray, Alice. 2010. 'Leadership in a Network of Communities: A Phenomenographic Study'. *The Learning Organization: An International Journal* 17 (1): 24–40.
4 Heifetz and Laurie. 2001. 'The Work of Leadership'.
5 Cressey, Peter. 2006. 'Collective Reflection and Learning: From Formal to Reflective Participation'. In *Productive Reflection at Work*, edited by David Boud, Peter Cressey, and Peter Docherty, 68–80. London:

Routledge.; Ellström, Per-Erik. 2006. 'The Meaning and Role of Reflection in Informal Learning at Work'. In *Productive Reflection at Work*, edited by David Boud, Peter Cressey, and Peter Docherty, 57–67. Routledge.

6   Tucker, Anita L, Amy C Edmondson, and Steven Spear. 2002. 'When Problem Solving Prevents Organizational Learning'. *Journal of Organizational Change Management* 15 (2): 122–37.

7   Hunt, Osborn, and Boal. 2009. 'The Architecture', 508.

34   Culture

1   Schein, Edgar H. 2010. *Organizational Culture and Leadership*. 4th ed. Vol. 2. John Wiley & Sons., 7-9.

2   Ibid

3   Hofstede, Geert. 1993. 'Cultural Constraints in Management Theories'. *Academy of Management Perspectives* 7 (1): 81–94., 89.

4   Szulanski, Gabriel. 1996. 'Exploring Internal Stickiness: Impediments to the Transfer of Best Practice within the Firm'. *Strategic Management Journal* 17 (S2): 27–43.; Whelan, Chad. 2016. 'Organisational Culture and Cultural Change: A Network Perspective'. *Australian & New Zealand Journal of Criminology* 49 (4): 583–599.

5   Hofstede 1993. 'Cultural Constraints', 89.

6   King, William R. 2007. 'A Research Agenda for the Relationships between Culture and Knowledge Management'. *Knowledge and Process Management* 14 (3): 226–36. https://doi.org/10.1002/kpm.281.

7   Schneider, Benjamin, Mark G Ehrhart, and William H Macey. 2013. 'Organizational Climate and Culture'. *Annual Review of Psychology* 64: 361–388. 10.1146/annurev-psych-113011-143809.

8   Yu, Chien, Tsai-Fang Yu, and Chin-Cheh Yu. 2013. 'Knowledge Sharing, Organizational Climate, and Innovative Behavior: A Cross-Level Analysis of Effects'. *Social Behavior and Personality: An International Journal* 41 (1): 143–156., 152.

9   Schneider, Ehrhart and Macey. 2013. 'Organizational climate'.

10   Yu, Yu, and Yu 2013. 'Knowledge Sharing'.

11   Ribiere and Sitar. 2003. 'Critical role'.

12   King 2007. 'A Research Agenda'.

13   Ibid

14   Hinds, Pamela J, and Jeffrey Pfeffer. 2003. 'Why Organizations Don't "Know What They Know": Cognitive and Motivational Factors Affecting

the Transfer of Expertise'. In *Sharing Expertise: Beyond Knowledge Management*, edited by Mark Ackerman, Volkmar Pipek, and Volker Wulf, 3–26. Cambridge MA: MIT Press, 15.

15 Leonard, Dorothy A. 2011. *Managing Knowledge Assets, Creativity and Innovation.* Singapore: World Scientific Publishing Co Pte Ltd., 272.

16 Schneider, Ehrhart and Macey. 2013. 'Organizational climate'.

17 De Long and Fahey. 2000. 'Diagnosing Cultural Barriers'.

18 King 2007. 'A Research Agenda'.

36 Risk

1 Antonacopoulou, Elena. 2000. 'Employee Development through Self-Development in Three Retail Banks'. *Personnel Review* 29 (4): 491–97.; Pedler, Mike, John Burgoyne, and Tom Boydell. 2013. *A Manager's Guide to Self-Development.* McGraw-Hill Education (UK).

37 Awareness

1 Richardson, Kurt, and Paul Cilliers. 2001. 'What Is Complexity Science? A View from Different Directions'. *Emergence, A Journal of Complexity Issues in Organizations and Management* 3 (1): 5–23.

2 Henning, Pamela Buckle, and Sloane Dugan. 2007. 'Leaders' Detection of Problematic Self-Organized Patterns in the Workplace'. In *Complex Systems Leadership Theory New Perspectives from Complexity Science on Social and Organizational Effectiveness*, edited by James K. Hazy, Jeffrey A. Goldstein, and Benyamin B. Lichtenstein, 1:387–414. ISCE Publishing.

3 DeMeritt, E Gordon. 2005. 'An Examination of the Effect of Organizational Storytelling on the Administrative Climate of Church-Based Schools as a Model for the Leadership of Nonprofit Organizations'. PhD Thesis, Capella University.
http://search.proquest.com/docview/305359141.

38 Knowledge Management

1 Drucker 1999. 'Knowledge-Worker Productivity', 79.

2 Alavi, Maryam, and Dorothy E Leidner. 2001. 'Knowledge Management and Knowledge Management Systems: Conceptual Foundations and Research Issues'. *MIS Quarterly*, 107–136.; Zack, Michael H. 1999. 'Developing a Knowledge Strategy'. *California Management Review* 41 (3): 125–145.

3   Adegbesan, J Adetunji. 2009. 'On the Origins of Competitive Advantage: Strategic Factor Markets and Heterogeneous Resource Complementarity'. *Academy of Management Review* 34 (3): 463–475.; Cohen, Wesley M, and Daniel A Levinthal. 1990. 'Absorptive Capacity: A New Perspective on Learning and Innovation'. *Administrative Science Quarterly* 35: 128–52.

4   Fahey and Prusak. 1998. 'The Eleven Deadliest'.

5   Zack, 1999. 'Managing Codified'.

6   uit Beijerse, Roelof P. 2000. 'Knowledge Management in Small and Medium-Sized Companies: Knowledge Management for Entrepreneurs'. *Journal of Knowledge Management* 4 (2): 162–79.

7   Yu, Yu, and Yu 2013. 'Knowledge Sharing'.

8   Moitra, Deependra, and Kuldeep Kumar. 2007. 'Managed Socialization: How Smart Companies Leverage Global Knowledge'. *Knowledge and Process Management* 14 (3): 148–57. https://doi.org/10.1002/kpm.278.

9   Nonaka 1991. 'The Knowledge-Creating'.

10   McAdam, Rodney, and Renee Reid. 2000. 'A Comparison of Public and Private Sector Perceptions and Use of Knowledge Management'. *Journal of European Industrial Training* 24 (6): 317–29.

11   Mason, David, and David J Pauleen. 2003. 'Perceptions of Knowledge Management: A Qualitative Analysis'. *Journal of Knowledge Management* 7 (4): 38–48.

12   McAdam and Reid. 2000. 'A Comparison of Public'.

13   Kalkan 2008. 'An Overall View'.

14   Demarest, Marc. 1997. 'Understanding Knowledge Management'. *Long Range Planning* 30 (3): 321–384.; McAdam and Reid. 2000. 'A Comparison of Public'; Perez, Jesus Rodriguez, and Patricia Ordóñez de Pablos. 2003. 'Knowledge Management and Organizational Competitiveness: A Framework for Human Capital Analysis'. *Journal of Knowledge Management* 7 (3): 82–91.; uit Beijerse 2000. 'Knowledge Management'.

15   McAdam and Reid. 2000. 'A Comparison of Public'.

16   Kalkan 2008. 'An Overall View'.

17   Ibid

18   Torugsa, Nuttaneeya Ann, and Wayne O'Donohue. 2016. 'Progress in Innovation and Knowledge Management Research: From Incremental to Transformative Innovation'. *Journal of Business Research* 69 (5): 1610–1614. https://doi.org/10.1016/j.jbusres.2015.10.026.

19 Füllan, Michael. 2014. *Leading in a Culture of Change, Personal Action Guide and Workbook*. CA 94104: Jossey-Bass.
20 Nahapiet and Ghoshal. 1998. 'Social Capital'.
21 Quinn, James Brian, Philip Anderson, and Sydney Finkelstein. 1996. 'Leveraging Intellect'. *Academy of Management Perspectives* 10 (3): 7–27. ; Hung, Shin-Yuan, Alexandra Durcikova, Hui-Min Lai, and Wan-Mei Lin. 2011. 'The Influence of Intrinsic and Extrinsic Motivation on Individuals' Knowledge Sharing Behavior'. *International Journal of Human-Computer Studies* 69 (6): 415–427.
22 Zack, 1999. 'Managing Codified'.

39 Organisational Knowledge
1 King, William R, and Dong-Gil Ko. 2001. 'Evaluating Knowledge Management and the Learning Organization: An Information/Knowledge Value Chain Approach'. *Communications of the Association for Information Systems* 5 (1): 14. http://aisel.aisnet.org.dbgw.lis.curtin.edu.au/cais/.
2 Argyris, Chris. 1976. 'Single-Loop and Double-Loop Models in Research on Decision Making'. *Administrative Science Quarterly* 21 (3): 363–75.; Peeters, Aaron, and Viviane Robinson. 2015. 'A Teacher Educator Learns How to Learn from Mistakes: Single and Double-Loop Learning for Facilitators of in-Service Teacher Education'. *Studying Teacher Education* 11 (3): 213–227.
3 Argyris 1976. 'Single-Loop and Double-Loop'.
4 Ibid; Peeters and Robinson. 2015. 'A Teacher Educator'.
5 Argyris 1976. 'Single-Loop and Double-Loop'; Argyris, Chris. 1977. 'Double Loop Learning in Organizations'. *Harvard Business Review* 55 (5): 115–125.; Argyris, Chris. 1976. 'Theories of Action That Inhibit Individual Learning.' *American Psychologist* 31 (9): 638.
6 Argyris 1976. 'Single-Loop and Double-Loop'.
7 Argyris 1977. 'Double loop learning'; Argyris, Chris, and Donald A Schön. 1996. *Organizational Learning II: A Theory of Action Perspective*. 2nd ed. Wesley Publishing Company.
8 Argyris, Chris. 2003. 'A Life Full of Learning'. *Organization Studies* 24 (7): 1178–1192, 1184; Drew, Stephen A. W., and Peter A. C. Smith. 1995. 'The New Logistics Management'. *Logistics Information Management* 8 (1): 24–33. https://doi.org/10.1108/09576059510078729.

9   Sharpe and Long. 2012. 'Innovation in Canadian'.
10 Fahey and Prusak. 1998. 'The Eleven Deadliest'.
11 Yahyapour, Shiva, Mehdi Shamizanjani, and Mohammad Mosakhani. 2015. 'A Conceptual Breakdown Structure for Knowledge Management Benefits Using Meta-Synthesis Method'. *Journal of Knowledge Management* 19 (6): 1295–1309.
12 Osborn, Richard N., and James G. (Jerry) Hunt. 2007. 'Leadership and the Choice of Order: Complexity and Hierarchical Perspectives near the Edge of Chaos'. *The Leadership Quarterly* 18: 319–40. https://doi.org/10.1016/j.leaqua.2007.04.003.
13 Mednick, Sarnoff. 1962. 'The Associative Basis of the Creative Process.' *Psychological Review* 69 (3): 220–32. http://citeseerx.ist.psu.edu/viewdoc/download?doi=10.1.1.170.572&rep=rep1&type=pdf., 221.
14 Ibid, 224.
15 Zohar 1997. *Rewiring the Corporate, 35.*
16 Mitchell, Chris J, Jan De Houwer, and Peter F Lovibond. 2009. 'The Propositional Nature of Human Associative Learning'. *Behavioral and Brain Sciences* 32 (2): 183–246.
17 Rosas, Juan M, Travis P Todd, and Mark E Bouton. 2013. 'Context Change and Associative Learning'. *Wiley Interdisciplinary Reviews: Cognitive Science* 4 (3): 237–244.
18 Kang, Minhyung, and Mi-Jung Lee. 2017. 'Absorptive Capacity, Knowledge Sharing, and Innovative Behaviour of R&D Employees'. *Technology Analysis & Strategic Management* 29 (2): 219–232.
19 Cohen and Levinthal. 1990. 'Absorptive Capacity'.
20 Nelson, Richard R, and Sidney G. Winter. 1982. *An Evolutionary Theory of Economic Change.* Cambridge MA: Harvard University Press, 125.
21 Linderman, Pesut, and Disch. 2015. 'Sense Making'.
22 Burnard, Pamela. 2013. 'Leadership Creativities and Leadership Development in Higher Music Education'. In *Developing Creativities in Higher Music Education: International Perspectives and Practices*, 213. Oxon, UK: Routledge.; Kang and Lee. 2016. 'Absorptive Capacity'.
23 Cohen and Levinthal. 1990. 'Absorptive Capacity'.
24 Waddell and Pio. 2015. 'The influence of'.
25 Senge, Peter M. 1990. 'The Leader's New Work: Building Learning Organizations'. *Sloan Management Review* 32 (1): 17–23., 8

26 Chambers, Foulon, Handfield-Jones, Hankin, and Michaels. 1998. 'The War for Talent.'

27 Wang, Catherine L, and Pervaiz K Ahmed. 2003. 'Organisational Learning: A Critical Review'. *The Learning Organization* 10 (1): 8–17., 15.

28 Dieckhoff, Martina. 2013. 'Continuing Training in Times of Economic Crisis'. In *Economic Crisis, Quality of Work, and Social Integration: The European Experience*, edited by Duncan Gallie. Oxford University Press.; Drew and Smith. 1995. 'The New Logistics Management'.

29 Hsu and Fang. 2009, 'Intellectual Capital'; Wang and Ahmed. 2003. 'Organisational Learning'.

40 Tacit Knowledge

1 Spulber, Daniel F. 2012. 'Tacit Knowledge with Innovative Entrepreneurship'. *International Journal of Industrial Organization* 30 (6): 641–653.; Quinn, Robert, Sue Faerman, Michael Thompson, and Michael McGrath. 2003. *Becoming a Master Manager: A Competency Framework*. Third. John Wiley & Sons, Inc.

2 Sánchez, Judit Hernández, Yolanda Hernández Sánchez, Daniel Collado-Ruiz, and David Cebrián-Tarrasón. 2013. 'Knowledge Creating and Sharing Corporate Culture Framework'. *Procedia - Social and Behavioral Sciences* 74: 388–97. https://doi.org/10.1016/j.sbspro.2013.03.029.

3 Dicken 2015. *Global shift, 108.*

4 Kalkan 2008. 'An Overall View'.

5 Kakabadse, Nada K., Alexander Kouzmin, and Andrew Kakabadse. 2001. 'From Tacit Knowledge to Knowledge Management: Leveraging Invisible Assets'. *Knowledge and Process Management* 8 (3): 137–154.

6 Nonaka 1991. 'The Knowledge-Creating'.

7 Staw, Barry M, and Robert I Sutton. 2000. *Research in Organizational Behavior*. 1st ed. Vol. 22. JAI Press.

8 Grote 2005. *Forced Ranking, 31*; Ulrich 1998. 'Intellectual Capital', 18.

9 Hester, John. 2013. 'The High Cost of Employee Turnover and How to Avoid It'. *Nonprofit World* 31 (3): 20–21. ; Staw 1980. 'The Consequences of Turnover.'

10 Moitra and Kumar. 2007. 'Managed socialization'.

11 Gurteen 1998. 'Knowledge'; Shalley, Gilson, and Blum. 2009. 'Interactive Effects'.

12 Gurteen 1998. 'Knowledge'; Kohn and Smith. 2011. 'Collaborative Fixation'.

13 Vallacher, Robin R, and Andrzej Nowak. 1998. *Dynamical Social Psychology*. New York, NY: The Guilford Press.

14 Abelson, Robert P. 1979. 'Social Clusters and Opinion Clusters'. In *Perspectives on Social Network Research*, edited by Paul W. Holland and Samuel Leinhardt, 239–256. Academic Press Inc., 247; Kalargiros, Emmanuel M, and Michael R Manning. 2015. 'Divergent Thinking and Brainstorming in Perspective: Implications for Organization Change and Innovation', Research in Organizational Change and Development'. In *Research in Organizational Change and Development*, 23:293–327. Emerald Group Publishing Limited. .

15 Kalargiros and Manning. 2015. 'Divergent Thinking'; Vallacher and Nowak. 1998. *Dynamical Social Psychology.*

16 Bies, Robert J., Jean M. Bartunek, Timothy L. Fort, and Mayer N. Zald. 2007. 'Corporations as Social Change Agents: Individual, Interpersonal, Institutional, and Environmental Dynamics'. *Academy of Management Review* 32 (3): 788–93. .

17 Park, Hoon, Sun Dai Hwang, and J Kline Harrison. 1996. 'Sources and Consequences of Communication Problems in Foreign Subsidiaries: The Case of United States Firms in South Korea'. *International Business Review* 5 (1): 79–98. http://www.sciencedirect.com.dbgw.lis.curtin.edu.au/science/article/pii/0969593196000340#.

18 Moran, Robert T, Neil Remington Abramson, and Sarah V Moran. 2014. *Managing Cultural Differences*. 9th ed. Oxon, UK: Routledge.

19 Martins, Ellen C, and Fransie Terblanche. 2003. 'Building Organisational Culture That Stimulates Creativity and Innovation'. *European Journal of Innovation Management* 6 (1): 64–74.; Sinclair, Amanda. 1993. 'Approaches to Organisational Culture and Ethics'. *Journal of Business Ethics* 12 (1): 63–73.; Smith, Aaron CT, and Bob Stewart. 2011. 'Organizational Rituals: Features, Functions and Mechanisms'. *International Journal of Management Reviews* 13 (2): 113–133.

20 Ogbonna, Emmanuel, and Lloyd C Harris. 2002. 'Managing Organisational Culture: Insights from the Hospitality Industry'. *Human Resource Management Journal* 12 (1): 33–53.; Ibid.

21 Sinclair 1993. 'Approaches to Organisational', 66.

22 Bovens, Mark. 2007. 'Analysing and Assessing Accountability: A Conceptual Framework 1'. *European Law Journal* 13 (4): 447–468.
23 Nahapiet and Ghoshal. 1998. 'Social Capital'.

41 Emergent Properties
1   Parker, Philip D, John Jerrim, Ingrid Schoon, and Herbert W Marsh. 2016. 'A Multination Study of Socioeconomic Inequality in Expectations for Progression to Higher Education: The Role of between-School Tracking and Ability Stratification'. *American Educational Research Journal* 53 (1): 6–32.
2   Capra, Fritjof, and Pier Luigi Luisi. 2014. *The Systems View of Life: A Unifying Vision.* Original. Cambridge University Press.; Case, Jennifer M. 2015. 'Emergent Interactions: Rethinking the Relationship between Teaching and Learning'. *Teaching in Higher Education* 20 (6): 625–635.; Uhl-Bien, Marion and McKelvey. 2007. 'Complexity Leadership Theory'.
3   Bak, Per, Chao Tang, and Kurt Wiesenfeld. 1987. 'Self-Organized Criticality: An Explanation of the 1/f Noise'. *Physical Review Letters* 59 (4): 381–84. https://doi.org/10.1103/PhysRevLett.59.381.; Chiles, Todd H, Alan D Meyer, and Thomas J Hench. 2004. 'Organizational Emergence: The Origin and Transformation of Branson, Missouri's Musical Theaters'. *Organization Science* 15 (5): 499–519.; Kauffman, Stuart A. 1993. *The Origins of Order: Self-Organization and Selection in Evolution.* Oxford University Press.; Prehofer, Christian, and Christian Bettstetter. 2005. 'Self-Organization in Communication Networks: Principles and Design Paradigms'. *IEEE Communications Magazine* 43 (7): 78–85.; Uhl-Bien and Marion. 2009. 'Complexity Leadership in Bureaucratic'; Case 2015. 'Emergent Interactions'.
4   Lichtenstein, Benyamin B, and Donde Ashmos Plowman. 2009. 'The Leadership of Emergence: A Complex Systems Leadership Theory of Emergence at Successive Organizational Levels'. *The Leadership Quarterly* 20: 617–30..
5   Hazy, James K., Jeffrey A Goldstein, and Benyamin B Lichtenstein. 2007. *Complex Systems Leadership Theory New Perspectives from Complexity Science on Social and Organizational Effectiveness.* Edited by James K. Hazy, Jeffrey A Goldstein, and Benyamin B Lichtenstein. Vol. 1. Mansfield: ISCE Publishing..
6   Hazy, James K, and Mary Uhl-Bien. 2015. 'Towards Operationalizing

Complexity Leadership: How Generative, Administrative and Community-Building Leadership Practices Enact Organizational Outcomes'. *Leadership* 11 (1): 79–104.

7 Ibid.
8 Marion, Russ. 2008. 'Complexity Theory for Organizations and Organizational Leadership'. In *Complexity Leadership Part 1: Conceptual Foundations*, edited by Mary Uhl-Bien and Russ Marion, 1–13. IAP - Information Age Publishing, Inc.
9 Case 2015. 'Emergent Interactions'; Ibid.
10 Bright, Margaret. 2011. 'An Examination of Adaptive Leadership Processes Using Action Research'. PhD Thesis, Graduate School: Clemson University.; ii.
11 Ibid
12 Marion and Uhl-Bien 2001. 'Leadership in Complex Organisations'.
13 Marion 2008. 'Complexity Theory'.
14 Uhl-Bien, Marion and McKelvey. 2007. 'Complexity Leadership Theory'.
15 Uhl-Bien and Marion. 2009. 'Complexity Leadership in Bureaucratic'.
16 Shinbrot, Troy. 1994. 'Synchronization of Coupled Maps and Stable Windows'. *Physical Review E* 50 (4): 3230.; Smiraglia, Richard P, and Charles van den Heuvel. 2013. 'Classifications and Concepts: Towards an Elementary Theory of Knowledge Interaction'. *Journal of Documentation* 69 (3): 360–83.
17 Nowak, Andrzej, Robin R. Vallacher, and Michal Zochowski. 2005. 'The Emergence of Personality: Dynamic Foundations of Individual Variation'. *Developmental Review* 25 (3): 351–85.
18 Capra and Luisi. 2014. *The Systems View of Life*; Case 2015. 'Emergent Interactions'; Uhl-Bien, Marion and McKelvey. 2007. 'Complexity Leadership Theory'.
19 Nowak, Vallacher and Zochowski. 2005. 'The Emergence of Personality'; Vallacher and Nowak. 1998. *Dynamical Social Psychology.*
20 Pikovsky, Arkady, Michael Rosenblum, and Jürgen Kurths. 2003. *Synchronization: A Universal Concept in Nonlinear Sciences*. Vol. 12. Cambridge university press.,15-17.

42 Emergence
1 Chiles, Meyer and Hench. 2004. 'Organizational Emergence'.
2 Schneider, Marguerite, and Mark Somers. 2006. 'Organizations as

Complex Adaptive Systems: Implications of Complexity Theory for Leadership Research'. *The Leadership Quarterly* 17 (4): 351–65. https://doi.org/10.1016/j.leaqua.2006.04.006.
3   Schreiber and Carley. 2006. 'Leadership Style'.
4   Kauffman 1993. *The Origins of Order, 393.*
5   Panzar, Hazy, McKelvey and Schwandt. 2007. 'The Paradox'.
6   Heifetz, Grashow and Linsky. 2009. *The Practice of Adaptive Leadership*
7   Uhl-Bien and Marion. 2009. 'Complexity Leadership in Bureaucratic'.
8   Marion 2008. 'Complexity Theory'.

Part Six: Social Capital

1   Leana and Van Buren III. 1999. 'Organizational Social Capital'.
2   Subramaniam, Mohan, and Mark A Youndt. 2005. 'The Influence of Intellectual Capital on the Types of Innovative Capabilities'. *Academy of Management Journal* 48 (3): 450–463.
3   Ibid
4   Leana and Van Buren III. 1999. 'Organizational Social Capital'.
5   Burt, Ronald S. 2009. *Structural Holes: The Social Structure of Competition.* Harvard university press.
6   Smelser, Neil J. 1997. *Problematics of Sociology: The Georg Simmel Lectures, 1995.* Univ of California Press,xii.
7   Bies, Bartunek, Fort and Zald. 2007. 'Corporations as Social Change',789.
8   Miner, John B. 2005. *Organizational Behavior 1: Essential Theories of Motivation and Leadership.* Vol. 1. NY: Routledge.

43 Meso
1   Bies, Bartunek, Fort and Zald. 2007. 'Corporations as Social Change',789.
2   Uhl-Bien, Marion and McKelvey. 2007. 'Complexity Leadership Theory'.
3   Kilduff, Martin, and Wenpin Tsai. 2003. *Social Networks and Organizations.* London: Sage.,88.
4   Albert, Réka, and Albert-László Barabási. 2000. 'Topology of Evolving Networks: Local Events and Universality'. *Physical Review Letters* 85 (24): 5234. http://link.aps.org/doi/10.1103/PhysRevLett.85.5234.
5   Kilduff, Martin, Craig Crossland, and Wenpin Tsai. 2008. 'Pathways of Opportunity in Dynamic Organizational Networks'. In *Complexity Leadership Part I: Conceptual Foundations*, edited by Mary Uhl-Bien and Russ Marion, 1:83–99. Charlotte, NC: IAP - Information Age Publishing,

Inc.

6   Klonsky, Melinda. 2010. 'Discussing Undiscussables: Exercising Adaptive Leadership'. Fielding Graduate University.

7   Nahapiet and Ghoshal. 1998. 'Social Capital'.

8   Leana and Van Buren III. 1999. 'Organizational Social Capital'.

9   Granovetter 1973. 'The Strength of Weak Ties'.

44 Macro

1   Spada, Cosimo. 2007. 'Bureaucratic Agents: Simulating Organizational Behavior and Hierarchical Decision-Making'. In *Complex Systems Leadership Theory New Perspectives from Complexity Science on Social and Organizational Effectiveness*, edited by James K. Hazy, Jeffrey A. Goldstein, and Benyamin B. Lichtenstein, 1:247–70. ISCE Publishing.

2   Kauffman 1993. *The Origins of Order.*

3   Miner 2015. *Organizational Behavior 1.*

4   Spada 2007. 'Bureaucratic Agents'.

5   Prigogine, Ilya, and Isabelle Stengers. 1997. *The End of Certainty: Time, Chaos and the New Laws of Nature*. New York, NY: The Free Press.

6   Plowman and Duchon. 2007. 'Emergent Leadership'.

7   Uhl-Bien and Marion. 2009. 'Complexity Leadership', 340.

8   Bartos, Paul J. 2007. 'Is Mining a High-Tech Industry?: Investigations into Innovation and Productivity Advance'. *Resources Policy* 32 (4): 149–158.

45 Diversity

1   Erbe, Nancy D. 2014. *Approaches to Managing Organizational Diversity and Innovation*. Hershey PA, USA: IGI Global., XV

2   Zubielqui, Graciela Corral de, Janice Jones, and Larissa Statsenko. 2016. 'Managing Innovation Networks for Knowledge Mobility and Appropriability: A Complexity Perspective'. *Entrepreneurship Research Journal* 6 (1): 75–109. https://doi.org/10.1515/erj-2015-0016.

3   Humala, Iris Annukka. 2015. 'Leadership toward Creativity in Virtual Work in a Start-up Context'. *Journal of Workplace Learning* 27 (6): 426–41.

4   Heifetz and Laurie. 2001. 'The Work of Leadership'; Friedel, Curtis. 2014. 'The Value of Adaption and Innovation as a Function of Diversity'. In *Approaches to Managing Organizational Diversity and Innovation*, edited by Nancy D Erbe, 63–81. Hershey PA, USA: IGI Global.

5   Friedel 2014. 'The Value of Adaption'.
6   Will, Thomas E. 2016. 'Flock Leadership: Understanding and Influencing Emergent Collective Behavior'. *The Leadership Quarterly* 27 (2): 261–279.
7   Hofhuis, Joep, Pernill GA Van Der Rijt, and Martijn Vlug. 2016. 'Diversity Climate Enhances Work Outcomes through Trust and Openness in Workgroup Communication'. *SpringerPlus* 5 (1): 714.
8   Poutanen, Petro, Kalle Siira, and Pekka Aula. 2016. 'Complexity and Organizational Communication: A Quest for Common Ground'. *Human Resource Development Review* 15 (2): 182–207.
9   Moitra and Kumar. 2007. 'Managed Socialization'.
10   Mazur, Barbara. 2010. 'Cultural Diversity in Organisational Theory and Practice'. *Journal of Intercultural Management* 2 (2): 5–15.
11   Sawyer, Katina. 2015. 'International Perspective'. In *The Oxford Handbook of Workplace Discrimination*, edited by Adrienne J. Colella and Eden B. King. Oxford University Press, USA.
12   Hofstede 1993. 'Cultural Constraints', 92.
13   Tange, Hanne, and Jakob Lauring. 2009. 'Language Management and Social Interaction within the Multilingual Workplace'. *Journal of Communication Management* 13 (3): 218–32. https://doi.org/10.1108/13632540910976671.
14   Jonasson and Lauring. 2012. 'Cultural Differences'.
15   Costa Jr, Paul T, and Robert R McCrae. 2013. 'The Five-Factor Model of Personality and Its Relevance to Personality Disorders'. Edited by Steven Hyman. *Personality and Personality Disorders: The Science of Mental Health* 7: 17.; Goldberg, Lewis R. 1993. 'The Structure of Phenotypic Personality Traits.' *American Psychologist* 48 (1): 26–34.
16   McAdams, Dan P, and Jennifer L Pals. 2006. 'A New Big Five: Fundamental Principles for an Integrative Science of Personality.' *American Psychologist* 61 (3): 204–17., 204.
17   Dhir, Krishna S, and Abíódún Gòkè-Paríolá. 2002. 'The Case for Language Policies in Multinational Corporations'. *Corporate Communications: An International Journal* 7 (4): 241–51.
18   McAdams and Pals. 2006. 'A New Big Five', 204.
19   Jonasson and Lauring. 2012. 'Cultural Differences'.
20   Tange and Lauring. 2009. 'Language Management'.

Part Seven: Relational Capital

46 Characteristics
1 Starovic and Marr. 2003. 'Understanding Corporate Value'.
2 Bolino, Turnley and Bloodgood. 2002. 'Citizenship Behaviour'.
3 Caroline Martins and Meyer 2012. 'Organizational and behavioural'; Ulrich 1998. 'Intellectual Capital'.
4 Uhl-Bien and Marion. 2009. 'Complexity Leadership'.
5 Bolino, Turnley and Bloodgood. 2002. 'Citizenship Behaviour'.

47 Managed Socialisation
1 Marion, Russ, Jon Christiansen, Hans W Klar, Craig Schreiber, and Mehmet Akif Erdener. 2016. 'Informal Leadership, Interaction, Cliques and Productive Capacity in Organizations: A Collectivist Analysis'. *The Leadership Quarterly* 27 (2): 242–260.
2 Bolino, Turnley and Bloodgood. 2002. 'Citizenship Behaviour'.
3 Moitra and Kumar. 2007. 'Managed Socialization'.
4 Ibid
5 Richards, Deborah, and Peter Busch. 2013. 'Knowing-Doing Gaps in ICT: Gender and Culture'. *Vine* 43 (3): 264–95.
6 Nahapiet and Ghoshal. 1998. 'Social Capital'.
7 Kang and Lee. 2016. 'Absorptive Capacity'.
8 Evans, Evan Carl. 2013. 'The Effects of Organizational Leadership and Culture on Tacit Knowledge Utilization'. PhD Thesis, Lawrence Technological University.
9 Marion, Christiansen, Klar, Schreiber, and Erdener. 2016. 'Informal Leadership', 245.
10 Groggins, Ashley, and Ann Marie Ryan. 2013. 'Embracing Uniqueness: The Underpinnings of a Positive Climate for Diversity'. *Journal of Occupational and Organizational Psychology* 86 (2): 264–282.
11 Marion, Christiansen, Klar, Schreiber, and Erdener. 2016. 'Informal Leadership'.
12 Poutanen, Siira, and Aula. 2016. 'Complexity and Organizational'.

48 Agential Interactions
1 Plowman and Duchon. 2007. 'Emergent Leadership'.
2 Zubielqui, Jones, and Statsenko. 2016. 'Managing Innovation Networks'.
3 Marion and Uhl-Bien. 2001. 'Leadership in Complex Organisations'.

4   Ibid
5   Uhl-Bien and Marion. 2009. 'Complexity Leadership in Bureaucratic Forms'.
6   Hazy and Uhl-Bien. 2015. 'Towards operationalizing', 80.
7   Goldspink, Christopher, and Robert Kay. 2010. 'Emergence In Organizations: The Reflexive Turn'. *E:CO* 12 (3): 47–73., 48.
8   Liang 2015. 'Relativistic Complexity'; Maturana, Humberto R, and Francisco J Varela. 1980. *Autopoiesis and Cognition: The Realization of the Living*. Vol. 42. Dordrecht, Holland: D.Reidel Publishing Company.
9   Will 2016. 'Flock Leadership'.
10 Anderson, Philip. 1999. 'Complexity Theory and Organization Science'. *Organization Science* 10 (3): 216–32.
11 Zubielqui, Jones, and Statsenko. 2016. 'Managing Innovation Networks'.
12 Harter, Nathan. 2007. 'Leadership as the Promise of Simplification'. In *Complex Systems Leadership Theory New Perspectives from Complexity Science on Social and Organizational Effectiveness*, edited by James K. Hazy, Jeffrey A. Goldstein, and Benyamin B. Lichtenstein, 1:333–48. ISCE Publishing.
13 Surie and Hazy. 2006. 'Generative Leadership'.
14 Marion, Christiansen, Klar, Schreiber, and Erdener. 2016. 'Informal Leadership'.
15 Borzillo and Kaminska-Labbé. 2011. 'Unravelling the Dynamics'.
16 Uhl-Bien, Marion and McKelvey. 2007. 'Complexity Leadership Theory'.
17 Anderson. 1999. 'Complexity Theory'; Prehofer, Christian, and Christian Bettstetter. 2005. 'Self-Organization in Communication Networks: Principles and Design Paradigms'. *IEEE Communications Magazine* 43 (7): 78–85.
18 Poutanen, Siira, and Aula. 2016. 'Complexity and Organizational'.
19 Lichtenstein, Benyamin B, Mary Uhl-Bien, Russ Marion, Anson Seers, James Douglas Orton, and Craig Schreiber. 2006. 'Complexity Leadership Theory: An Interactive Perspective on Leading in Complex Adaptive Systems'. *E:CO* 8 (4): 2–12.
20 Yukl 1999. 'An Evaluation of'.
21 Denis, Jean-Louis, Ann Langley, and Viviane Sergi. 2012. 'Leadership in the Plural'. *Academy of Management Annals* 6 (1): 211–283.
22 Zubielqui, Jones, and Statsenko. 2016. 'Managing Innovation Networks'.

49 Interactions
1 Pfeffer 1985. 'Organizational Demography'.
2 Schreiber and Carley. 2006. 'Leadership Style'
3 Plowman and Duchon. 2007. 'Emergent Leadership'.
4 Schreiber and Carley. 2006. 'Leadership Style'.
5 Uhl-Bien and Marion. 2009. 'Complexity Leadership',632.
6 Panzar, Hazy, McKelvey and Schwandt. 2007. 'The Paradox'.
7 Schwandt, David R. 2008. 'Individual and Collective Coevolution'. In *Complexity Leadership Part 1: Conceptual Foundations*, edited by Mary Uhl-Bien and Russ Marion, 101–127. IAP - Information Age Publishing, Inc.
8 Uhl-Bien and Marion. 2009. 'Complexity Leadership'.
9 Janis, Irving Lester. 1972. *Victims of Groupthink: A Psychological Study of Foreign-Policy Decisions and Fiascoes.* Houghton Miffin Company.
10 Panzar, Hazy, McKelvey and Schwandt. 2007. 'The Paradox'.
11 Pfeffer 1985. 'Organizational Demography'.
12 Wanberg, John, Amy Javernick-Will, Paul Chinowsky, and John E Taylor. 2015. 'Spanning Cultural and Geographic Barriers with Knowledge Pipelines in Multinational Communities of Practice'. *Journal of Construction Engineering and Management* 141 (4): 04014091.
13 Lin, Iris Y, and Catherine T Kwantes. 2015. 'Potential Job Facilitation Benefits of "Water Cooler" Conversations: The Importance of Social Interactions in the Workplace'. *The Journal of Psychology* 149 (3): 239–262.
14 Plowman and Duchon. 2007. 'Emergent Leadership'.
15 Ibid
16 Anderson 1999. 'Complexity Theory'; Runco, Mark A. 2014. *Creativity: Theories and Themes: Research, Development, and Practice.* 2nd ed. Elsevier.
17 Moitra and Kumar. 2007. 'Managed Socialization'.

50 Generative Relationships
1 Carmeli, Abraham, Daphna Brueller, and Jane E Dutton. 2009. 'Learning Behaviours in the Workplace: The Role of High-Quality Interpersonal Relationships and Psychological Safety'. *Systems Research and Behavioral Science: The Official Journal of the International Federation for Systems Research* 26 (1): 81–98; Lane, David, and Robert Maxfield. 1996.

'Strategy under Complexity: Fostering Generative Relationships'. *Long Range Planning* 29 (2): 215–31.

2   Uhl-Bien, Marion and McKelvey. 2007. 'Complexity Leadership Theory'.

3   Linderman, Pesut, and Disch. 2015. 'Sense Making'.

4   Surie and Hazy. 2006. 'Generative Leadership'.

5   Anzoise, Valentina, and Stefania Sardo. 2016. 'Dynamic Systems and the Role of Evaluation: The Case of the Green Communities Project'. *Evaluation and Program Planning* 54: 162–172.

6   Rouse, William B. 2008. 'Health Care as a Complex Adaptive System: Implications for Design and Management'. *Bridge-Washington-National Academy of Engineering-* 38 (1): 17.

7   Burrell, Gibson, and Gareth Morgan. 1979. 'Sociological Paradigms and Organisational Analysis: Elements of the Sociology of Corporate Life'. In *Complex Systems Leadership Theory New Perspectives from Complexity Science on Social and Organizational Effectiveness,* edited by James K Hazy, Jeffrey A. Goldstein, and Benyamin B. Lichtenstein. ISCE Publishing.

8   Denhardt, Robert B. 1989. *In the Shadow of Organization.* University Press of Kansas.

9   Rudolph, Michael. 2008. *Ritual Performances as Authenticating Practices: Cultural Representations of Taiwan's Aborigines in Times of Political Change.* Vol. 14. LIT Verlag Münster.

10 Stahl, Günter K, Martha L Maznevski, Andreas Voigt, and Karsten Jonsen. 2010. 'Unraveling the Effects of Cultural Diversity in Teams: A Meta-Analysis of Research on Multicultural Work Groups'. *Journal of International Business Studies* 41 (4): 690–709.

51 Networks

1   Skilton, Paul F, Robert M Wiseman, and William H Glick. 2011. 'Managing For Impact in Business Research Programs: Scope and Collaboration'. In *Current Topics in Management: Global Perspectives on Strategy, Behavior, and Performance*, edited by Afzalur M. Rahim, 1:179. NJ: Transaction Publishers; 183; Ulrich 1998. 'Intellectual Capital'; 17

2   Asah, Stanley T, and Dale J Blahna. 2012. 'Motivational Functionalism and Urban Conservation Stewardship: Implications for Volunteer Involvement'. *Conservation Letters* 5 (6): 470–477.

52 Communication
1   Lichtenstein, Uhl-Bien, Marion, Seers, Orton and Schreiber. 2006. 'Complexity Leadership Theory'.
2   Plowman, Donde Ashmos, and Dennis Duchon. 2008. 'Dispelling the Myths about Leadership: From Cybernetics to Emergence'. *Complexity Leadership Part* 1: 129–153, 138.
3   Marion and Uhl-Bien. 2001. 'Leadership in Complex', 392.
4   Preiser, Rika, and Paul Cilliers. 2010. 'Unpacking the Ethics of Complexity: Concluding Reflections'. In *Complexity, Difference and Identity*, 265–287. Netherlands: Springer, 268.
5   Uhl-Bien and Marion. 2009. 'Complexity Leadership in Bureaucratic'
6   Lord 2008. 'Beyond Transactional'.
7   Uhl-Bien and Marion. 2009. 'Complexity Leadership in Bureaucratic'
8   Lichtenstein, Uhl-Bien, Marion, Seers, Orton and Schreiber. 2006. 'Complexity Leadership Theory', 3.
9   Holland, John H, and John H Miller. 1991. 'Artificial Adaptive Agents in Economic Theory'. *American Economic Review* 81 (2): 365–72.
10 White, Leroy, Graeme Currie, and Andy Lockett. 2016. 'Pluralized Leadership in Complex Organizations: Exploring the Cross Network Effects between Formal and Informal Leadership Relations'. *The Leadership Quarterly* 27 (2): 280–297.
11 Zubielqui, Jones, and Statsenko. 2016. 'Managing Innovation Networks'
12 Chin, Jean Lau, Lyne Desormeaux, and Katina Sawyer. 2016. 'Making Way for Paradigms of Diversity Leadership.' *Consulting Psychology Journal: Practice and Research* 68 (1): 49.
13 Allen, Gloor, Colladon, Woerner, and Raz. 2016. 'The Power of Reciprocal'.
14 Uhl-Bien and Marion. 2009. 'Complexity Leadership in Bureaucratic'
15 Hunt, Osborn, and Boal. 2009. 'The Architecture'.
16 Surie and Hazy. 2006. 'Generative Leadership'.
17 Carmeli, Brueller, and Dutton. 2009. 'Learning Behaviours'; Lane and Maxfield. 1996. 'Strategy under Complexity'.
18 Surie and Hazy. 2006. 'Generative Leadership'.
19 Holland and Miller. 1991. 'Artificial Adaptive Agents'.
20 Anderson 1999. 'Complexity Theory'; Prehofer and Bettstetter. 2005. 'Self-Organization'.
21 Litaker, David, Anne Tomolo, Vincenzo Liberatore, Kurt C. Stange, and

David Aron. 2006. 'Using Complexity Theory to Build Interventions That Improve Health Care Delivery in Primary Care'. *J Gen Intern Med* 21 Suppl 2: S30-4. https://doi.org/10.1111/j.1525-1497.2006.00360.x.

22 Rotmans, Jan, and Derk Loorbach. 2009. 'Complexity and Transition Management'. *Journal of Industrial Ecology* 13 (2): 184–97.

23 Anderson 1999. 'Complexity Theory'; Prehofer and Bettstetter. 2005. 'Self-Organization'.

24 Surie and Hazy. 2006. 'Generative Leadership'.

25 Lichtenstein and Plowman. 2009. 'The Leadership of'.

26 Starovic, and Marr. 2003. 'Understanding Corporate Value'.

27 Canadian International Council 2014. 'The 9 Habits'.

28 Ogle, Richard. 2007. *Smart World: Breakthrough Creativity and the New Science of Ideas.* Harvard business school press.

29 Bandura, Albert. 1999. 'Social Cognitive Theory: An Agentic Perspective'. *Asian Journal of Social Psychology* 2 (1): 21–41.;10.

30 Heifetz, and Laurie. 2001. 'The Work of Leadership'.

31 Geyer, Felix, and Johannes van der Zouwen. 1986. *Sociocybernetic Paradoxes: Observation, Control and Evolution of Self-Steering Systems.* London: SAGE Publications Ltd.

32 Maturana, and Varela. 1980 *Autopoiesis and Cognition*, xxvi.

33 Ibid

53 Thin Communication

1   Bjørge, Anne Kari. 2014. 'Discourse Strategies for Cross-Cultural Communication'. In *Global Leadership Practices: A Cross-Cultural Management Perspective*, edited by Bettina Gehrke and Marie-Thérèse Claes, 67–81. Palgrave Macmillan; Park, Hoon, Sun Dai Hwang, and J Kline Harrison. 1996. 'Sources and Consequences of Communication Problems in Foreign Subsidiaries: The Case of United States Firms in South Korea'. *International Business Review* 5 (1): 79–98.

2   Bjørge, Anne Kari, and Sunniva Whittaker. 2014. 'Language Management'. In *Global Leadership Practices: A Cross-Cultural Management Perspective*, edited by Bettina Gehrke and Marie-Thérèse Claes, 51–66. Palgrave Macmillan; Park, Hwangt, and Harrison. 1996. 'Sources and Consequences'.

3   Nonaka 1991. 'The Knowledge-Creating'.

4   Ibid

5   Plowman and Duchon. 2007. 'Emergent Leadership'.
6   Jonasson and Lauring. 2012. 'Cultural Differences'.

54   Essentialism
1   Parsons, Talcott. 1991. *The Social System*. Psychology Press.
2   Ibid, 385
3   Breunlin, Douglas C, William Pinsof, and William P Russell. 2011.
     'Integrative Problem-Centered Metaframeworks Therapy I: Core Concepts
     and Hypothesizing'. *Family Process* 50 (3): 293–313; Rousseau, Denise
     M. 1990. 'Normative Beliefs in Fund-Raising Organizations: Linking
     Culture to Organizational Performance and Individual Responses'. *Group
     & Organization Studies* 15 (4): 448–460.
4   Fishbein, Martin, and Icek Ajzen. 1975. *Belief, Attitude, Intention, and
     Behavior: An Introduction to Theory and Research*. Addison-Wesley;
     Knudson-Martin, Carmen, and Anne Rankin Mahoney. 2009. 'Introduction
     to the Special Section—Gendered Power in Cultural Contexts'. *Family
     Process* 48 (1): 5–8.
5   Parsons 1951. *The Social System*; Jonasson and Lauring. 2012. 'Cultural
     Differences'.
6   Kaya, Ayhan. 2005. 'Cultural Reification in Circassian Diaspora:
     Stereotypes, Prejudices and Ethnic Relations'. *Journal of Ethnic and
     Migration Studies* 31 (1): 129–149, 144.
7   Wilson, Gail. 2001. 'Conceptual Frameworks and Emancipatory Research
     in Social Gerontology'. *Ageing and Society* 21 (4): 471–487.
     https://doi.org/10.1017/S0144686X01008315.
8   Hatch and Cunliffe. 2013. *Organization Theory*.; Nicholson, Nigel, Randall
     Schuler, Andrew H. Van De Ven, Cary Cooper, and Chris Argyris, eds.
     1995. *The Blackwell Encyclopedic Dictionary of Organizational Behavior*.
     Blackwell Publishers Ltd.
9   Heifetz, Ronald A, and Marty Linsky. 2004. 'When Leadership Spells
     Danger'. *Educational Leadership* 61 (7): 33–37.

Part Eight: Adaptive Leadership

1   Plowman and Duchon. 2007. 'Emergent Leadership'.
2   Tang, Fangcheng. 2011. 'Knowledge Transfer in Intra-Organization
     Networks'. *Systems Research and Behavioral Science* 28 (3): 270–282.
3   Lichtenstein, Uhl-Bien, Marion, Seers, Orton and Schreiber. 2006.

'Complexity Leadership Theory'.
4 Hatch and Cunliffe. 2013. *Organization Theory.*
5 Nonaka 1991. 'The Knowledge-Creating', 97.
6 Kauffman 1993. *The Origins of Order.*
7 Herbert, Simon A. 1956. 'Rational Choice and the Structure of the Environment.' *Psychological Review* 63 (2): 129.
8 Lichtenstein, Uhl-Bien, Marion, Seers, Orton and Schreiber. 2006. 'Complexity Leadership Theory'.
9 Heifetz and Laurie. 2001. 'The Work of Leadership'.
10 Uhl-Bien, Marion and McKelvey. 2007. 'Complexity Leadership Theory'
11 Ibid
12 Ibid
13 Buber, Martin. 2003. *Between Man and Man.* Florence, KY, USA: Routledge, X.
14 Bradbury, Hilary, and Benyamin B. Lichtenstein. 2000. 'Relationality in Organisational Research: Exploring The Space Between'. *Organization Science* 11 (5): 551.
15 Uhl-Bien, Marion and McKelvey. 2007. 'Complexity Leadership Theory'
16 Mendes, Maria, Catarina Gomes, Pedro Marques-Quinteiro, Pedro Lind, and Luís Curral. 2016. 'Promoting Learning and Innovation in Organizations through Complexity Leadership Theory'. *Team Performance Management* 22 (5/6): 301–9; Osborn and Hunt. 2007. 'Leadership and the'; Uhl-Bien and Marion. 2009. 'Complexity Leadership in Bureaucratic'.
17 Plowman and Duchon. 2007. 'Emergent Leadership'.
18 Heifetz, Grashow, and Linsky. 2009. *The Practice of Adaptive Leadership.*
19 Bolino, Turnley and Bloodgood. 2002. 'Citizenship Behaviour'.
20 Lichtenstein, Uhl-Bien, Marion, Seers, Orton and Schreiber. 2006. 'Complexity Leadership Theory'.
21 Hatch and Cunliffe. 2013. *Organization Theory.*
22 Marion and Uhl-Bien. 2001. 'Leadership in Complex Organisations'
23 Lichtenstein, Uhl-Bien, Marion, Seers, Orton and Schreiber. 2006. 'Complexity Leadership Theory'.
24 Dess and Shaw. 2001. 'Voluntary Turnover, Social Capital', 447.

55 Innovation

1 Nonaka 1991. 'The Knowledge-Creating', 97.

2	Dewar, Robert D, and Jane E Dutton. 1986. 'The Adoption of Radical and Incremental Innovations: An Empirical Analysis'. *Management Science* 32 (11): 1422–1433; Norman, Donald A, and Roberto Verganti. 2014. 'Incremental and Radical Innovation: Design Research vs. Technology and Meaning Change'. *Design Issues* 30 (1): 78–96; Slater, Stanley F, Jakki J Mohr, and Sanjit Sengupta. 2014. 'Radical Product Innovation Capability: Literature Review, Synthesis, and Illustrative Research Propositions'. *Journal of Product Innovation Management* 31 (3): 552–566.

3	Ettlie, John E. 1983. 'Organizational Policy and Innovation among Suppliers to the Food Processing Sector'. *Academy of Management Journal* 26 (1): 27–44; Norman and Verganti. 2014. 'Incremental and Radical Innovation'.

4	Starovic and Marr. 2003. 'Understanding Corporate Value'.

5	Santos, Amalia, and Mark Stuart. 2003. 'Employee Perceptions and Their Influence on Training Effectiveness'. *Human Resource Management Journal* 13 (1): 27–46.

6	Keep, Ewart. 1989. 'A Training Scandal'. *Personnel Management in Britain*, 177–202.

7	Pemberton, Jonathan D, and George H Stonehouse. 2000. 'Organisational Learning and Knowledge Assets - An Essential Partnership'. *The Learning Organization* 7 (4): 184.

8	Rowley, Jennifer. 2000. 'From Learning Organisation to Knowledge Entrepreneur'. *Journal of Knowledge Management* 4 (1): 7.

9	Canadian International Council 2014. 'The 9 Habits', 26.

**56	Attractors**
1	Vallacher and Nowak. 1998. *Dynamical Social Psychology*, Chap 2.

2	Ibid

3	Hunt, Osborn, Boal. 2009. 'The Architecture'.

4	Boal and Schultz. 2007. 'Storytelling, Time, and Evolution', 413.

5	Cîndea, Ion. 2006. 'Complex Systems–New Conceptual Tools for International Relations'. *Perspectives: Review of Central European Affairs* 14 (1): 46–68.

6	Kanamaru, Takashi, Hiroshi Fujii, and Kazuyuki Aihara. 2013. 'Deformation of Attractor Landscape via Cholinergic Presynaptic Modulations: A Computational Study Using a Phase Neuron Model'. *PLoS One* 8 (1): e53854.

7   Dubinskas, Frank A. 1994. 'On the Edge of Chaos: A Metaphor for Transformative Change'. *Journal of Management Inquiry* 3 (4): 355–366; Losada, Marcial, and Emily Heaphy. 2004. 'The Role of Positivity and Connectivity in the Performance of Business Teams: A Nonlinear Dynamics Model'. *American Behavioral Scientist* 47 (6): 740–765; Warren-Adamson, Chris, and Julia Stroud. 2015. 'Using Complexity Theory in Kinship Practice'. *Child & Family Social Work* 20 (4): 407–414.
8   Losada and Heaphy. 2004. 'The Role of Positivity'.
9   Vallacher and Nowak. 1998. *Dynamical Social Psychology*, 59.
10 Lord 2008. 'Beyond Transactional'.
11 Vallacher and Nowak. 1998. *Dynamical Social Psychology*
12 Haigh, Carol. 2002. 'Using Chaos Theory: The Implications for Nursing'. *Journal of Advanced Nursing* 37 (5): 462–469, 464.

57 Identity and Tension
1   Lichtenstein, Uhl-Bien, Marion, Seers, Orton and Schreiber. 2006. 'Complexity Leadership Theory'.
2   Plowman and Duchon. 2007. 'Emergent Leadership'.

58 Resonate
1   Hunt, Osborn, Boal. 2009. 'The Architecture'.
2   Osborn and Hunt. 2007. 'Leadership and the'.
3   Uhl-Bien and Marion. 2009. 'Complexity Leadership in Bureaucratic'
4   Stein 1953. 'Creativity', 318.
5   Grant, Adam M, and James W Berry. 2011. 'The Necessity of Others Is the Mother of Invention: Intrinsic and Prosocial Motivations, Perspective Taking, and Creativity'. *Academy of Management Journal* 54 (1): 73–96, 74.
6   Marion and Uhl-Bien. 2001. 'Leadership in Complex Organisations'.
7   Ibid, 396.

59   Summary
1   Levy 2011. 'Knowledge Retention'.
2   Jonasson, and Lauring. 2012. 'Cultural Differences'.
3   Stahl, Maznevski, Voigt, and Jonsen. 2010. 'Unraveling the Effects'
4   Morrison 2011. 'Employee Voice Behavior', 405.

60 Opportunities for Research
1   Cabrita and Bontis. 2008. 'Intellectual Capital'; Hitt, Michael A. 1998. 'Twenty-First Century Organisations: Business Firms, Business Schools and the Academy'. *Academy of Management Review* 23 (2): 218.
2   Prewitt, Vana. 2004. 'Integral Leadership for the 21 St Century'. *World Futures* 60 (4): 327–333, 328.
3   Mendes, Gomes, Marques-Quinteiro, Lind, and Curral. 2016. 'Promoting Learning'.
4   Allen, Gloor, Colladon, Woerner, and Raz. 2016. 'The Power of Reciprocal'.
5   Zubielqui, Jones, and Statsenko. 2016. 'Managing Innovation Networks'.
6   Borzillo and Kaminska-Labbé. 2011. 'Unravelling the Dynamics'.
7   Surie and Hazy. 2006. 'Generative Leadership'.
8   Hofhuis, Rijt, and Vlug. 2016. 'Diversity Climate'; Moitra and Kumar. 2007. 'Managed Socialization'.
9   Kalkan 2008. 'An Overall View'.

Part Nine: Conclusion and Recommendations

61 Theoretical Application
1   Plowman and Duchon. 2007. 'Emergent Leadership'.
2   Kanungo 2001. 'Ethical Values'.
3   Plowman and Duchon. 2007. 'Emergent Leadership'.
4   Ibid
5   Lord 2008. 'Beyond Transactional'.
6   Plowman and Duchon. 2007. 'Emergent Leadership'.
7   Heifetz, Grashow, and Linsky. 2009. *The Practice of Adaptive Leadership.*
8   Bolino, Turnley and Bloodgood. 2002. 'Citizenship Behaviour'.
9   Moitra and Kumar. 2007. 'Managed Socialization'.
10 Surie and Hazy. 2006. 'Generative Leadership', 18.
11 Starovic and Marr. 2003. 'Understanding corporate value', 20; Uhl-Bien and Marion. 2009. 'Complexity Leadership in Bureaucratic', 645.
12 Surie and Hazy. 2006. 'Generative Leadership',18.
13 Starovic and Marr. 2003. 'Understanding Corporate Value', 20.
14 Uhl-Bien and Marion. 2009. 'Complexity Leadership in Bureaucratic', 645.

63 Limitations

1 Jonasson and Lauring. 2012. 'Cultural Differences'.
2 Borzillo and Kaminska-Labbé. 2011. 'Unravelling the Dynamics'.
3 Surie and Hazy. 2006. 'Generative Leadership'.
4 Moitra and Kumar. 2007. 'Managed Socialization'.
5 Kalkan 2008. 'An Overall View'.

Index

J

K

Acknowledgements

||Om Gan Ganpataye Namo Namaha||

I am deeply grateful to my dad: my role model for portraying essential values to adopt. Mum, your daily and unconditional support mean the world to me. I love you and am forever indebted to you both. You have supported me through many efforts and failures to mould me into the man I am today.

My brother Rajesh and Sister-In-Law Nireksha, your support through challenging times has brought immense relief and is hugely appreciated. I thank you for your continued presence and guidance. My nephews Chirag and Yash, you impress me with your achievements and down to earth presence. Thank you for being so grounded, focused and for making the family proud with your accomplishments.

Bin, your unconditional friendship and understanding is a blessing for which I am deeply indebted. I thank you for your consistent presence. Joy, you are my voice of reason, spiritual guidance and importantly, a very dear friend. Your critique and suggestions have inspired and encouraged innovative thinking. I thank you.

Numerous individuals, including all my reviewers, have initiated enlightenment and inner peace. My sincere thanks and appreciation to you all.

Terminology

1. **Complexity leadership theory**. Addresses the dynamic and adaptive behaviours of interdependent agents who interact within systems under conditions of internal and external pressures.[1]

2. **Adaptive leadership**. An informal leadership process that occurs in the interactions of interdependent agents, generating and advancing innovative solutions to adaptive challenges.[2]

3. **Intellectual capital management**. The management of knowledge assets attributed to an organisation, which significantly contribute to and improve its sustainability and competitive position.[3]

4. **Transient or Transient mobile workforce**. All non-core employees including subcontractors, outsourced jobs, consultants, part-time, fixed-term, temporary, casual or home employment conditions.[4]

5. **Social capital**. An asset rooted in the relationships of individuals, communities, networks or societies.[5]

6. **Transient Social Capital**. Social capital that emanates and flourishes from the use of a transient or transient mobile workforce within the organisation.

7. **Complex Adaptive System (CAS)**. A system comprised of a multitude of persons, components or nodes, often referred to as agents, who interact to adapt and learn.[6]

8. **Functional participation**. Behaviours that go beyond the call of

duty to perform one's job; for example, undertaking additional duties or volunteering for special projects.[7]

9. **External mind.** Relationships and interactions with individuals outside the organisation, such as consultants, contractors, customers, suppliers and peers, to accumulate knowledge critical for competitive advantage.[8]

10. **Hyper-competition.**[9] An environment of increasingly volatile competition in which organisational benefits rapidly grow and diminish[10] to make these environments dynamic, unpredictable and hostile.[11]

11. **Agents or Agential.** All core organisational employees and staff.

About the Author

Dr Alkesh Vyas is the founder and principal of Micro Lens Consulting, a company offering support and clarity to businesses dealing with dynamic challenges such as cost efficiency, knowledge retention, creativity and competitiveness. With involvement in substantial systems improvement and an analytical, growth and creative mindset, he has facilitated over $50 Million in annual cost savings in international and Australian-based corporations. Alkesh also regularly shares views on his Instagram gallery @microlensc.

An active community contributor, Alkesh promotes growth for local businesses through strategy identification and development as well as serving meals at community events and providing transportation for volunteers. A seasoned photographer, he also offers comprehensive photography services for these community events and established Dhuleez Photography to provide a gamut of photography services and high-quality prints of his macro and landscape art images. A sample showcase is on display at www.dhuleez.com and his Instagram gallery @photos_av.

Alkesh recently started learning music and the acoustic guitar and can comfortably strum a few choice tunes. However, this might be a distressing experience for his audience!

Bibliography

1   Marion, Russ. 2008. 'Complexity Theory for Organizations and Organizational Leadership'. In *Complexity Leadership Part 1: Conceptual Foundations*, edited by Mary Uhl-Bien and Russ Marion, 1–13. IAP - Information Age Publishing, Inc.

2   Heifetz, Ronald A., and Donald L Laurie. 2001. 'The Work of Leadership'. *Harvard Business Review* 79 (11): 131–41.

3   Starovic, Danka, and Bernard Marr. 2003. 'Understanding Corporate Value: Managing and Reporting Intellectual Capital', May, 1–28. www.cimaglobal.com.

4   Horwitz, Frank M., Chan Teng Heng, and Hesan Ahmed Quazi. 2003. 'Finders, Keepers? Attracting, Motivating and Retaining Knowledge Workers'. *Human Resource Management Journal* 13 (4): 23–44. https://doi.org/10.1111/j.1748-8583.2003.tb00103.x.

5   Nahapiet, Janine, and Sumantra Ghoshal. 1998. 'Social Capital, Intellectual Capital, and the Organizational Advantage'. *Academy of Management Review* 23 (2): 242–67.

6   Holland, John H. 2006. 'Studying Complex Adaptive Systems'. *Journal of Systems Science and Complexity* 19 (1): 1–8. https://doi.org/10.1007/s11424-006-0001-z.

7   Bolino, Mark C, William H Turnley, and James M Bloodgood. 2002. 'Citizenship Behavior and the Creation of Social Capital in Organisations'. *Academy of Management Journal* 27 (4): 505–22. http://www.medwelljournals.com.

8   Nonaka, Ikujiro, and Hirotaka Takeuchi. 1995. *The Knowledge-Creating Company: How Japanese Companies Create the Dynamics of Innovation.* Oxford University Press.

9   Dicken, Peter. 2015. *Global Shift: Mapping The Changing Contours of The World Economy.* 7th ed. New York, NY: The Guildford Press, 118

10   D'Aveni, Richard A. 2010. *Hypercompetition: Managing the Dynamics of Strategic Manoeuvring.* NY: Simon and Schuster Inc, 2

11   D'Aveni, Richard A. 1995. 'Coping with Hypercompetition: Utilizing the New 7S's Framework'. *Academy of Management Perspectives* 9 (3): 45–57. https://doi.org/10.5465/ame.1995.9509210281.